KT-146-766

# Student Life:
# A Survival Guide

Withdrawn

T012426

Accession Number....24,727 ©

Class Number........374

## Acknowledgments

Anecdotes by: Daniel Bradbury, John Fitzpatrick (Aberystwyth University); Russell Beck (Bath University); Phil Mitchel (Bangor University); Ian Carter, Jon Dale, Barbara Murray, Alison Pinnock, Jon Roycroft, Michelle Stratford (Brighton University and the University of Sussex); Professor Kate Belsey (Cardiff University); Cherry Canovan (Durham University); Sharon Annette, Johnathan Clapham, Moira Fraser, John Travers (Edinburgh University); Clare Neill (Hull University); Kathy Cain (Kent University); Simon Cambell, Clyde Loakes, Andy White (Lampeter University); Stuart Feathers (Liverpool University); Mona Lisa Cook, Emma Parkinson, Andrew Todd (Loughborough University); Phil Stephenson (Nottingham Trent University); Gerard Roe (Oriel College, Oxford University); Tim Connolly, Anna Roberts (QMW, University of London); Bill Quinn (Queen's University, Belfast); Jane MacVikers (Salford University); Nic Gibson (SOAS, University of London); Ali Carslake, Jo Kimber, Adelle Robinson (Swansea University); Phil Agulnik, Chris Evans (UCL, University of London); Claire Wills (Wolverhampton University).

Editorial assistance: Phil Agulnik, Johnathan Clapham, Mona Lisa Cook, Tarn Lamb, Anna Roberts, Simon Tuttle, Claire Wills and welfare officers throughout the country.

Technical support: Nic Gibson of Interactive Europe with Sairer Coley and *London Student*, the student newspaper of the University of London.

Additional thanks to: Richard Marshall, National Union of Students (London), Cora Oldfield, Angela Wood and the lower sixth at Bedford High School.

# Student Life: A Survival Guide

**Natasha Roe**

Student Helpbook Series

HOBSONS

**CRAC**

 © Hobsons Publishing PLC 1994

ISBN 1 85324 827 4

A CIP catalogue record for this book is available from the British Library.

No part of this publication may be copied or reproduced, stored in a retrieval system or transmitted in any form or by any means electronic or mechanical or by photocopying, recording or otherwise without prior permission of the publishers.

## CRAC

The Careers Research and Advisory Centre (CRAC) is a registered educational charity. Hobsons Publishing PLC produces CRAC publications under exclusive licence and royalty agreements.

Printed and bound in Great Britain by Clays Ltd, Bungay, Suffolk.

Cover artwork by Jo Robinson
Text illustration by Tony Husband
Text design by Leah Klein

Ref L141/E/10/qq/C/JE

# Contents

# Introduction

So you've made the decision – you know what you want to study. But how are you going to get to college and where will you live? How are you going to feed yourself and stay healthy? Who's going to pay all the bills and keep the landlord happy? Are you going to plunge headlong into the social swim or get down to business in the library?

 I arrived at university wide-eyed at all the opportunities around me: masses of new friends; entertainment on tap; sports centre a short walk away; a bar in college and a key to my own door. I threw myself into college life and enjoyed every minute of it. The only facility I didn't use to the full was the library! If I had my time again, I think I'd try to tip the balance a bit more in favour of my course.

*Graduate, University of York*

Whether you're just leaving school or have worked for years before deciding to go on to further or higher education, whatever your particular needs or interests, *Student Life* will help you keep your head above the flood of decisions and pressures that face you now. This guide will lead you through the crucial first few weeks and help you make the most of the rest of your time at college or university; your home life, your course and your new social circle.

# 1 Money

The whole business of student finances has caused some pretty heated action in students' unions in recent years. The introduction of student loans and the removal of housing benefit and income support means that, as a full-time student, you are probably going to be poor for the duration of your course. However, most people will be in the same boat and, at the very least, living on a tight budget develops some valuable skills.

This chapter will tell you how to make sure you get all the money you are entitled to and give you tips on how to make the pennies stretch further.

## Grants, loans and access funds

### What is a grant?

The term 'mandatory grant' covers two payments. There is the payment given by your local education authority directly to your university which covers the cost of your tuition fee, and the maintenance payment which is the money you have to live on.

If you fulfil the criteria for grant eligibility, you automatically have your tuition fees paid. The maintenance grant is means-assessed: the higher your parents' incomes, the higher their contribution. The size of maintenance grant you are entitled to is judged on the combined 'residual income' of your parents for the previous year. Residual income means gross income less allowances for dependants, pension schemes, etc. For full details consult *Student Grants and Loans*, a free booklet published by the Department for Education.

### How much is your grant?

The following table shows the levels of maintenance funding you will be given if you are awarded a full grant. These figures do not include your tuition fees.

| Grant rates for 1994-95 | |
| --- | --- |
| **London** | £2,560 |
| **Elsewhere** | £2,040 |
| **Students living at home** | £1,615 |

Details of how levels of parental income affect your maintenance grant will be sent to you with your application form. Your parents will be asked to contribute to your maintenance grant if their combined residual income is over £14,840. They will be expected to pay for all of your maintenance if their combined residual income is greater than about £34,000. However, many parents do not pay their full contribution. You should make sure you send all the documentation asked for, as failing to do this will mean your grant is delayed or miscalculated.

We have real problems here on the south coast because we have London prices but without the London weighting.

*Welfare Officer, Brighton University*

The only way your maintenance grant will be judged on your own finances is if you are 26 or over or if you can prove that you have been financially independent for three years. You will usually have to get your parents to write a letter to the local authority saying that they have disowned you if you want to pursue this avenue.

If you are a married mature student then your grant will be means tested against your spouse's income. This is true if you are over 25. Under 25, you can still be married but your parents' incomes will be assessed. If you are single and 26 or over, you will receive an additional allowance to meet your living costs.

> It really annoys me that my husband's income means that I don't get any grant. I have been working and paying taxes for years and this seems really unfair. I also think it is biased against men as they tend to be the ones who have been able to get the jobs which pay the mortgage and this system is financially prohibitive to them going back into higher education.

*First-year student, Kent University*

## Who qualifies for a grant?

Everyone on a full-time course of higher education is entitled to receive a mandatory grant from his or her local education authority in England and Wales, the Scottish Education Department in Scotland and the Library and Education Boards in Northern Ireland. A full-time course of higher education is defined as one leading to a first degree, a Diploma of Higher Education, a Higher National Diploma, a teaching certificate, including the Postgraduate Certificate in Education (PGCE), or any course provided by a university which leads to certificates, diplomas or qualifications comparable with a degree. The latter includes the degree-type courses run by the Business and Technology Education Council (BTEC). To qualify you will also have to be 'ordinarily resident' in the UK for three years prior to the start of your course, which basically means you will have had to have been in the UK for some purpose other than tourism.

## Who doesn't qualify?

You are not eligible if you have studied on a higher education course before – unless you are going on to do a PGCE. This criterion might become important if you think of changing courses (see chapter 5 for details).

Also, if you are already employed and your employer gives you enough sponsorship to cover your tuition fees and your maintenance grant, you will not be given a local authority grant. You are, however, entitled to receive sponsorship up to a certain amount without losing your grant and should check with the authority responsible for allocating your grant for up-to-date details.

You can also be refused a grant if you have shown yourself to be 'unfit' to hold an award. You shouldn't worry about this though, even if you have a stack of unpaid parking fines or have been caught causing a public disturbance on a Saturday night, as there have been no cases reported of students being refused a grant on these grounds.

---

### WARNING !

↔ You will be refused a grant if you fail to fill in the forms on time so it is really important that you meet the deadline.

---

### Extra money you may be able to claim

There are certain circumstances under which you are able to claim additional allowances. You should contact the authority responsible for paying your grant if you think you fit any of the following criteria:

↔ you are required to study for longer than 30 weeks and three days (25 weeks and three days for Oxbridge students) and particularly if your course lasts for 45 weeks, then you should make sure you are receiving a grant for all 52 weeks of the year

↔ you have dependants or are a single parent

↔ you have a disability which means it is more expensive for you to study (see chapter 9 for details)

- ◆▸ you are training to be a teacher on a course lasting up to two years in a subject which currently needs more teachers (you should get details from TASC)
- ◆▸ you own two homes
- ◆▸ you are 26 or over.

You should also contact your LEA if your parents' status changes (for instance if they get divorced or retire) as the LEA should re-assess your claim and amend your grant allocation accordingly.

Scottish students can claim for any travel costs their course incurs above the £70 travel allowance included in their grant. Get a copy of the relevant form from the university or students' union if you want to claim for this, and make sure you keep an accurate record of all travel expenses.

If studying abroad is a requirement of your course then you can claim back the cost of any medical insurance or medical treatment you need while there.

### What to do if your grant cheque is late

I didn't get my grant until week ten and I never really recovered from that. That's why I ended up in so much debt.

*Second-year student, Loughborough University.*

This is a student's biggest nightmare and unfortunately is something that happens quite frequently. It is usually sorted out within a few weeks and banks are quite lenient, if you can provide them with proof that you have been awarded a grant. It is vital that you keep all documentation you are sent concerning your grant applications, and you should always double check, before you send off your grant forms, that you have filled out all the questions and included all the information requested.

If your grant is late then the first thing to check with the authority that is issuing your grant is that it has all the information it requires. Send any additional information immediately as the administration processes involved in clearing grant applications appear to be extremely long-winded at the best of times. Unfortunately the authorities are under no obligation to process your application within a certain time.

I see a lot of students with late grant problems in the first few weeks. It is usually quite a simple case of the LEA needing more information. If the student has photocopies of all communication I can sort any problems out much more quickly.

*Welfare Officer, Liverpool University*

If you do have to query anything with the LEA then make sure you take the name of the person you speak to. This can save valuable explanation time if you have further questions. If you need any help then go to your students' union as they will be only too used to dealing with the late arrival of grants.

## Student loans

This scheme was not at all popular with students' unions when it was introduced in 1990. The government decided to freeze maintenance grant levels, stop students from claiming housing benefit and income support and, instead, encourage them to borrow the difference. Student loans are now very much a part of student life and current students have little choice but to take out a loan.

The amount you are entitled to as a loan alters each year so check with your students' union or grant allocation authority for details.

| Loan rates for 1994–95 | | | |
|---|---|---|---|
| | London | Elsewhere | Students living at home |
| Full years | £1,375 | £1,150 | £915 |
| Final year | £1,005 | £840 | £670 |

**How to apply**

Student loans are administered by the Student Loans Company in Glasgow but you should go to your students' union in the first instance, as they will be able to tell you how to find the person responsible for processing loans in your university.

You will need to be under 50 years of age at the start of the course and on a full-time course of higher education leading to a first degree or equivalent (the only postgraduate course which qualifies is the PGCE). You will be given an eligibility questionnaire to fill out to check that you meet these criteria.

You will be asked for:

●▸ your birth certificate (or passport)

●▸ the letter from your local authority confirming your grant, if you have one

●▸ details of your bank or building society account because the money will be paid directly into, and the repayments taken out of, your account.

The college will then stamp your eligibility questionnaire and send it to the Student Loans Company which will send you an agreement that you will have to sign and return.

It depends on the time of year you apply but you will usually have to wait for a couple of months before your loan is fully processed. You can apply for a loan at any point in the academic year until the end of July. Remember that once you have applied for your loan you cannot take out another loan until the next academic year.

### Paying back your loan
Loan repayments begin in the April after you have finished your course. You can ask to defer your payments each year if your income is less than 85 per cent of the national average income at that time.

It is a really good idea to read all the communication you receive from the Student Loans Company carefully. I had so many debts when I left university I just gave the loan

letters a cursory glance. Bad idea. The first letter I got was one asking me whether I wanted to default on payments because my income was too low. The dole definitely counts as low income, in fact it is sub-survival money. It came as a bit of a shock therefore to find that £9.10 was automatically being taken out of my account – a huge proportion of the £33.60 I had to live on each week.

*Graduate, University of London*

When you do start repaying your loan, the money will be taken directly out of your bank account by automatic direct debit. Repayments will include the interest your loan has accumulated during your time of study and any deferment or default time. You cannot control the direct debit. The amounts you repay will be in roughly equal monthly instalments which will alter if the rate of interest alters. There are fixed periods when interest is reviewed and you will be told about these in advance.

Repayments will be over a fixed five-year period for courses lasting less than five years, and seven years for those courses lasting longer. Interest – which is index-linked to inflation – will be added. The rate is determined by the government each April. As an example, in the first year loans were introduced, repayment was at 9.8 per cent interest, and in the second year it was 5.8 per cent.

## To take a loan or not to take a loan

Many students refused to take out loans when they were first introduced as a protest against the scheme or because they didn't like the thought of being in debt when they left university. This is not now an option realistically open to students. The maintenance grant is so far behind the rate of inflation that stances of principle are out of the question.

All students are likely to be in debt at the end of their course and, although the banks will probably give you interest-free overdrafts while you are at university, they are not likely to be so lenient when you graduate. It might seem daunting to allow a company to debit money directly from your account but it is no worse than having a bank loan.

### Access funds

The access funds were introduced by the government to try to compensate for the state of increased poverty students were left in after they lost their entitlement to claim housing benefit, income support or dole, even during the holidays.

Access funds are sums of money given to universities to give to those students they feel are in need of financial assistance. To apply for an access fund you have to be a home, ie British, student studying on a full-time degree or sandwich course. Overseas students are not eligible.

Even if you fulfil these criteria you will not necessarily be given some money. It is entirely up to the individual universities how they allocate these funds and how much they give to each person.

Partly because there are no guidelines governing access funds you may hear some very unfair stories where one student who receives regular parental support has been given £500 and someone else with huge debts and no support has been refused financial help. These stories are becoming increasingly unusual, though, as colleges become more familiar with administering the funds.

To apply for an access fund you should go to your students' union to see if it has a list of your university's stipulations. The union or the registrar will tell you which department is dealing with access funds.

Do not feel embarrassed about accepting money in this way. The system is there to help you.

# What benefits can you claim?

The majority of students have been taken out of the benefit system altogether. There are also no longer provisions for parents to set up covenants to get tax rebates for the financial support they give their children. There are, however, limited groups of students who are entitled to claim state benefits. You may be entitled:

➡ if you are a lone parent

➡ if you have a disability (see chapter 9 for details).

Ask at your local benefit office for details if you fall into one of these categories.

# Sponsorship, charities and trusts

### Sponsorship

Getting someone to sponsor you through university is an excellent way of acquiring some much-needed extra funding. It can also give you very valuable insight into life outside higher education in the 'real' or working world. You should always apply well in advance and be prepared to write to many companies before you find one which is interested in you.

You stand a much better chance of being given sponsorship if you want to study pure or applied science or engineering. However, business and commerce-related subjects, such as economics, banking and accountancy can all attract sponsorship. If you are a humanities student sponsorship is probably not an option open to you unless you have very strong contacts with a large company. But you should not be afraid to ask. The worst that can happen is that they will say no. See the Lifesavers section on page 36 for details of directories which list companies that offer sponsorship.

## Company sponsorship

There are two main types of sponsorship. 'Employer-supported training' is when a company will give you extra money on top of your local education grant throughout your time at university. This will be combined with paid vacation work with your sponsor and, although there is not usually any formal agreement between sponsor and student, you may well be offered a job at the end of your course. However, you will not usually be committed to working for the company after your degree.

The most obvious advantage of sponsorship is money; not only the cash in hand but a summer job is usually guaranteed as well. This might not sound as glamorous as inter-railing

> or bumming around Greece but it does help
> to clear your overdraft and, believe you me,
> you'll have one. Perhaps more importantly it
> provides you with good work experience to
> boost your CV and, for engineering, it counts
> towards early entrance into a professional
> institution.

*Third-year student, Bath University*

The other form of sponsorship is a 'student apprentice-ship' where you are employed by a company which offers you a combination of in-house training and higher education courses.

It is possible to be sponsored for either a full-time or a sandwich course. In fact sandwich courses lend themselves particularly well to sponsorship, as part of the course requirement is that you spend some time in industry and you can probably arrange to do this with the firm that sponsors you. This was traditionally done under the 1:3:1 ratio (where you spend one year in industry, three years following a course of higher education, followed by a further year in industry) and this structure is well established in some universities. However, many sponsored students follow sandwich courses of a different structure or arrange to do any work as part of the sponsorship deal during the vacations.

> I turned down my sponsorship late in the day
> after the A-level results were out because of
> my moral dilemma about working for a
> company which accepted defence contracts.

*Third-year student, Bath University*

There are some disadvantages to being sponsored. Some companies will ask you to follow a particular course so you should consider whether this is the right one for you without being swayed too much by the prospect of extra cash. You should also find out how flexible or specific the courses or training schemes offered are and again make the right selection for you. It is also important to find out whether you will be bound to the company after you have completed your course.

**Sponsorship in the Armed Forces**
The Army, Navy and Air Forces also offer sponsorship for higher education courses under two different schemes:

1 bursaries
2 cadetships.

Bursaries are given each year to students who are interested in the Forces but who don't want to commit themselves immediately. If you are offered a cadetship, then you will join one of the Forces and be paid a salary while you are an undergraduate. You can apply for a cadetship either before you start university or during the first two years of your course. Under both schemes you will be expected to attend some training sessions at weekends for which you will be paid. The amount of time you will have to serve in the Force which has sponsored you varies according to whether you are awarded a cadetship or a bursary.

It was great. I had my student loan, my grant and £5,000 from the Army in my final year. The training weekends are a really good crack. You make lots of new friends and drink lots of beer while getting paid for the privilege. If you want to join the Forces then it is an incredibly good idea to be sponsored through university.

*President of the Students' Guild, Aberystwyth University*

Like other forms of sponsorship, the Forces tend to give preference to scientific and engineering courses, although subjects such as dentistry, medicine and catering are also considered. The emphasis is on your commitment to the Forces, so even if you are studying languages or other humanities your application may well be considered. However, the opportunities for men are greater than those for women. You should contact the schools or university liaison officer in your area for more information. The leaflet B1, *Graduates in the Forces* (published by Wiltshire Guidance Services), which is available from careers offices, may also be helpful to you.

## Charities and trusts

There are some charitable trusts from which it is possible to obtain funding for educational courses. There are many of these charities and most of them have very specific criteria you will need to meet before they give you any money. Some will only give funds to students who have already started a course and find they are not able to complete it because of a lack of money. If this is the case you will have to prove that you have explored all other avenues of funding before you approach them.

The amount you can get is also likely to be limited and is unlikely to be enough to fund an entire course, although it is possible to approach several organisations. If you do decide to approach a trust, make sure you have done your research thoroughly and can present your case well. Look at *The Directory of Charities*, produced by the Charities Aid Foundation, (see the Lifesavers section at the end of this chapter for further information).

# Paying your own way

Most students find that they need to work to supplement their grants and/or loans. The ways you can do this range from the exotic to the incredibly mundane – though when jobs are scarce, you may have to take whatever is offered.

You can make use of the need to work as a good way to build up your curriculum vitae (CV). The graduate job market is extremely competitive and is becoming more so as the number of graduates increases each year. Employers want work experience and evidence that you are interested in the job you are applying for, or at least some signs of initiative, so anything you can do to improve your chances while you are at university is extremely beneficial.

You don't necessarily need to work in the same field as your eventual career, but it is important that you do something that will give your prospective employer a good impression. For instance, if your ambition is to work in banking, running a holiday camp shows more leadership qualities than spending your holidays as a filing clerk in your local branch.

Whatever sort of job you apply for you are likely to need a CV. This is a record of your education and employment. You should include both your term-time and your home addresses, details of where you went to school, what exams you took (only include grades if they are outstanding), the dates and positions of any jobs you have had as well as your interests and any additional skills, such as computer literacy or a driving licence. You can also include any involvement you have had in university clubs and societies. If you don't feel your experience fits well into the traditional CV format then you may want to go for a prose style where you outline your suitability and keep the education and work details brief. However you present your CV, it should be typewritten and have perfect spelling and grammar.

If you have any doubts about how you should draw up a CV then there are books available in most careers libraries. *CVs and Applications* by Patricia McBride covers everything you need to know on this subject. It is £7.99 and available on 0403 710851. There are also specialist CV consultants who advertise in the local and national media, but don't forget that they will charge you for the service.

### Part-time work while studying

The part-time work available will, to a large extent, depend on where you are studying. You can find out what is available by looking in local newspapers, on newsagents' notice-boards, in employment agencies and JobCentres. Your students' union will also have information about local work and work within the union. Many students' unions actively try to provide as many jobs as possible for their students. This is usually bar work, shop work or security work but it can also be the place where budding DJs get their first break.

I was employed in my students' union as a
glass collector until a member of the rugby
club came up and asked me for a Tetleys. As
a foreign student, Tetleys meant tea to me so
I told him we didn't sell tea in the bar and he
would have to go upstairs. After that they
kept me behind the bar, where apparently I
could do less damage.

*Undergraduate, now Welfare Officer, Loughborough University*

You can also try advertising your services. You may be
lucky and be able to use your degree subject to offer
coaching and tuition. Anxious parents are often willing to
pay high hourly rates for the security of knowing their
child is receiving one-to-one tuition. But you could also
advertise your baby-sitting, dog-walking, typing, domestic or DIY services. Local newsagents don't charge much
to place an advertisement in their window and it is a good
way of capturing the local market.

I worked as a gardener during the summer
term of my first year. I went and knocked on
the door of a house I thought could probably
afford a gardener and definitely needed one
and the owners said yes. It was the best job I
have ever had. I could pick my own hours, I
would only work when the weather was good
and I was doing something I really enjoyed.
Ace.

*Second-year student, University of London*

You should be very careful about taking on too much outside work during term time. It is possible to balance both
but you will need to be very well organised (see chapter 5).

A survey conducted by the South East Area of the National Union of Students found that students who undertook more than 15 hours of paid work per week dropped by one grade in their final degree mark.

## Vacation work

Working during the holidays is a much better option if you want to leave yourself free to participate fully in undergraduate life. You will also have a better chance of getting the sort of jobs that are useful CV builders. You should remember that there will be masses of students all looking for employment during the vacations. Therefore you should try to get something sorted out well before term finishes so you get a head start.

"You'll probably be driving a transit van," Ken from the employment agency told me. When I turned up at the depot I saw two vehicles, a transit van and a 16 ton lorry-type thing. It was the 16 ton lorry-type thing I had to take on an epic journey along country lanes from Bristol to Dorset, Devon and Cornwall and back again delivering batteries. I certainly got to see the rugged scenery of the South West and learnt Radio One's playlist off by heart. The next day was the South Wales experience.

*Third-year student, University of London*

For some students, what they do in the holidays will already be determined. Those who are sponsored, for example, will probably be given vacation work as part of the sponsorship arrangement. You should not, however, assume that because you set up a sponsorship arrangement eight months ago, provisions will automatically have been made for your placement. You should ring your contact well before term finishes to discuss the situation and finalise any details. This will also show that you are keen to take them up on their offer.

I have the best vacation job ever. I work in Glasgow Airport on the information desk, which basically means I get paid £6.30 per hour for watching breakfast TV and waiting for the enquiries to come in. Working at the airport has made me think about applying to the BA graduate training scheme when I finish.

*Third-year student, Edinburgh University*

For many students, getting work in the holidays is not so easy, especially if unemployment in the area is high. JobCentres and employment agencies tend to give preference to people who do not have a course to return to in a few months time. In this situation you should try approaching people for whom you have worked before, if you got on well with them. They may be able to give you bits and pieces to do. You should also look out for seasonal opportunities. The Post Office, for instance, employs extra workers during the Christmas period and there will be seasonal fruit-picking and harvesting work in rural areas. It is worth approaching leisure industries such as hotels, catering and sports centres as these too have seasonal employment which will fit in with student holidays. Try sending off speculative CVs to people you think might be able to offer you work, ringing them up and even calling door-to-door.

Ribena is made by students. I started off shoving blackcurrants into a mill. Exhausting, but I enjoy the camaraderie and relish the extra money. I work eight hours a day minimum and change shifts every week. After a couple of summers I became a skilled machine operator which means pressing a few buttons once in a while and reading a book in between times. Last summer I got through 14 novels. Although I will never touch anything with blackcurrant in, it is not a bad way of supplementing my grant and making new friends.

*Third-year student, University of London.*

## Working holidays

Working holidays can be very enjoyable and give you valuable experience. You probably won't earn very much, usually just enough to keep you while you are there and perhaps enough to pay for your travel to the next destination. Working holidays are unlikely to bring a smile to your bank manager's face but are great for seeing the world on a tight budget and building up your CV.

I went to America on a BUNAC scheme and worked in a girl scout camp as a general assistant. I was doing everything from comforting homesick brats to arranging events. It was absolutely the best time of my life. Hard work, but it paid for my flight, and my board and keep was free. I was then able to spend some time touring afterwards.

Student travel operators, your students' union or careers library will all have details of what is available. You can choose to do anything from fruit-picking, helping run children's camps or au pairing, to working on an archaeological dig.

I lived on a kibbutz for six months. Initially I had to get up at 6 am and go into the chicken house and grab a handful of chickens and take them to the place where they were koshered. For the rest of the time I had to get up even earlier and pull out every other sunflower from this field until 11 am because apparently they get overcrowded. After that I had time to myself. I think I shocked the locals by bringing Western values to their small and very sheltered community.

*Third-year student, Lampeter University.*

## Work experience and voluntary work

This obviously will not help you financially while you are at university but may well lead to a job that will pay off your debts after you leave. Many companies are happy to have students in on work experience schemes for two to four weeks.

Last summer I went and worked for a magazine on a work experience placement for two weeks. It was a really good way of seeing how a magazine was run and gave me some valuable CV fodder. It actually turned out to be quite lucrative as well because a month later they needed someone who knew how the computers operated to lay out one of their publications so I was able to get a month's paid work.

*Second-year student, University of London.*

Write to or ring the company you are interested in working for and ask them whether they run work experience schemes. If they do offer you the opportunity, take the trouble to make a good impression. Do not be late, take long lunch breaks or give your friends the telephone number. They definitely won't offer you a job if you are unreliable.

Voluntary work can be very stimulating and often impresses prospective employers. If you have a specific

LIBRARY
BISHOP BURTON COLLEGE
BEVERLEY HU17 8QG

skill you can offer then you should try contacting one of the smaller charities which is looking for volunteers, as they are more likely to give you an interesting project with greater responsibility. However, any charitable organisation is going to be very grateful for an extra pair of hands.

## Taxation

As a full-time student you do not have to pay tax on any part-time or vacation work providing you do not earn more than the single person's allowance (currently £3,445 a year). This is quite unlikely so you should be able to keep all your hard-earned pennies. You should tell your employer that you are a student and he or she will give you a P38(S) to fill out. If you do earn more than £3,445, then you will be taxed at 20 per cent for the first £2,500 you earn, and 25 per cent for anything over that.

Sandwich-year students will be taxed at the full rate but your placement will probably run either side of the tax year (1 April to 31 March) so you may be able to claim some tax back when you finish. Final-year students will also be taxed at the normal rate for any work they do after they graduate. If you end up doing a series of temporary jobs and have not been working for the full financial year you may be able to claim tax back.

If you have come from employment back into education then you will be able to claim back the additional tax you will have paid while working, as tax levels are set on the assumption you will be working for the whole financial year. Get hold of form P50 and contact your local tax office or tax enquiry centre if you need any help.

# Budgeting

Do not be fooled by the relatively large sum of money deposited in your bank account at the beginning of term. When you break this down into weekly amounts and realise that it has to last you for the whole term, and possibly the vacation, all of a sudden it seems very small.

You will hear tales of students who blew their entire grant in the first few weeks and had to live in abject poverty for the rest of the term. They may well have had a great freshers' week but it is not worth it. Learning to manage your money is all part of leaving home and being able to live independently and you must account for the essentials before your grant cheque disappears across the bar.

> I didn't qualify for a full maintenance grant and my parents couldn't afford to give me the full parental contribution, although I got most of it. Living in London, this was particularly bad news. I survived because I was able to go home in the holidays and get reasonably well-paid temp work; but even so, I ended up with a £1,000 overdraft at the end of my second year. I don't think this pleased my bank manager too much because when I went to see him and told him I was doing an English degree and wanted to work in the media (a fatal admission), his response was to tell me that there was no way I would get a job and no I couldn't have any more money.

*Third-year student, University of London.*

The following are two sample budgets based on hypothetical students studying in Manchester and looking at their income and expenditure for the year. Their parental homes are a £25 return train fare away and they both work in the students' union bar during term time for £2.75 an hour. 'A' lives in a catered hall of residence within walking distance of the university, but has to buy lunch (a £1.20 sandwich and a 40p coffee from the students' union café) and goes back home in the vacations to live rent-free. Because of this, 'A' does not qualify for an access fund. 'B' rents a house in the private sector, an 80p return bus ride from the university, for the whole year, and has to meet utility and food bills during that time. 'B' qualifies for an access fund because 'B' rents in the private sector and this is one of the criteria the university has set.

| Sample budgets | | |
|---|---|---|
| **Income** | **A** | **B** |
| **Full grant and parental contribution** | £2,040 | £2,040 |
| **Student loan** | £1,150 | £1,150 |
| **Access fund** | —— | £150 |
| **Part-time work** | £635 | £635 |
| **Total** | £3,825 | £3,975 |
| **Expenditure** | **A** | **B** |
| **Rent** | £1,881 (£57 × 33) | £1,716 (£33 × 52) |
| **Bills** | —— | £250 |
| **Food** | £330 (£10 × 33) | £832 (£16 × 52) |
| **Travel** | £100 | £230 |
| **Books** | £200 | £200 |
| **Clothes** | £300 | £300 |
| **Travel home (four times a year)** | £100 | £100 |
| **Stationery** | £100 | £100 |
| **Laundry (twice a week)** | £66 | £104 |
| **Miscellaneous** (papers, entertainments, phone cards, etc) | £708 | £443 |
| **Total** | £3,825 | £4,275 |

On these budgets 'A' breaks even and 'B' has to use the £300 interest-free overdraft facility offered by the bank.

You should remember, that the calculations are based on the annual income and expenditure for these two sample students. You will have to draw up your own budget at the beginning of each term and may want to break it down into weekly budgets. 'A' has more available to spend on miscellaneous items because 'A' does not have to pay rent and food for the whole year. 'B' could only get a 52 week contract so stays in Manchester all year. 'B' therefore has to meet food and utilities bills for the whole year.

No one person's budget is likely to be the same as another's as we all have different priorities. Living in the private sector can be cheaper if you pare things down to a minimum. Just remember to allocate the money to rent, food, bills and travel before anything else.

### How to stick to your budget

Work out how much you have to spend each week. It is easier to keep track of what you are spending on a weekly basis than if you budget month by month. However, if you receive a monthly parental contribution cheque then a monthly budget makes more sense.

Once you have worked out what you need to spend on essentials, try to use your cheque book to pay for them, filling out the stubs each time. You will probably find that you are not left with much for the non-essentials. Divide whatever this turns out to be into weekly amounts and only take this amount of money out of the cash-point each week.

However careful you are you may find that there are times when the money isn't there to meet the bills. If this happens, do not panic. Prioritise where the money has to go and talk to your bank manager. Your rent, food and travel are all vital but remember, if you don't pay the bills of the utility companies they will cut you off and you will be landed with an extra reconnection charge.

Never sit on unopened bills or ignore letters demanding money. You should contact the people to whom you owe money immediately, as they are often prepared

to arrange other methods of payment. It is cheaper for them to allow you to pay over a period of time rather than to drag you through the courts. If you wait until things reach crisis point your finances will be much more difficult to sort out.

Again, if you need any help you should go to your students' union, the local Citizens' Advice Bureau or a debt counselling service. Whatever you do, DO NOT take out an unsecured loan. It is very easy to get these loans but the rates of interest the companies charge are crippling and you will end up in even greater debt. You should also avoid using credit cards unless you are sure you are disciplined enough to pay your bill promptly every month. It is very easy to run up large bills which you just can't pay when the demands come through, and the interest rates are outrageous.

## Rent

Rent is the largest sum of money you have to find from your funds and it must be a priority. If you live in a hall of residence then pay your fees AS SOON as you get your grant cheque. This large chunk of cheque is unlikely to be there at the end of term. If you pay your rent right at the start then you won't have to worry about it again.

If you live in a privately rented house then you might want to consider setting up a separate bank account for rent and bills. You can transfer the proportion of your grant cheque you need to cover this and not have to worry about finding the rent each month. You might also want to put money aside into a building society account to cover the bills. If you receive a monthly parental contribution then don't bother setting up two accounts, just pay your rent and bills the moment the money is in your account.

## Groceries

If you live somewhere where it is easy to get fresh food from markets or local shops, then it is much better for you nutritionally, and also for your pocket, if you buy food each day. If, however, the only option you have is to shop in a supermarket, then buy food weekly, keeping your eyes open for 'multi-buy' or 'special offers'. Write a weekly menu and buy only the ingredients you need. This reduces waste considerably. Buying in bulk and cooking in bulk also saves money, although you should make sure you store the food properly. You can also try going shopping late at night, especially on a Saturday, as many stores will reduce prices dramatically on goods approaching their 'use by' dates. However, bear in mind that if you buy fruit or vegetables that are not fresh they have little nutritional value.

As a general rule of thumb you should always try to buy fruit and veg from markets, meat from butchers and fish from fishmongers. It is amazing how much cheaper food is when it isn't wrapped in plastic – and the quality is often better. Always buy food that is in season. You can tell what is in season simply by looking at what is cheapest.

If you live in a shared house then you might find it is cheaper to buy food as a household. This will save arguments about whose loaf of bread you are eating but doesn't work so well if some members of the household eat considerably more than others.

Avoid buying prepared and processed food. It is much more expensive and you can prepare your own, more nutritional meals in the same time (see the Food section, chapter 3).

## Bills

The utility companies all offer a variety of payment schemes. You should choose the one you feel will suit you best and is easiest to manage. It is a good idea to arrange to have as many of your bills as possible paid by direct debit, with the money being taken directly out of your account. This will be more difficult if you live in a shared house although you can set up an account in the house's name. Contact the utility companies for details of the payment schemes they run.

## Clothes

Many students feel pressure to keep up with the latest fashion. You will not be able to afford to do this. Markets, second-hand shops and sales all offer cheaper alternatives to off-the-peg fashion items. If you can sew, then you could try making your own clothes.

## Books

You will be given a very long reading list when you are accepted onto your course. DO NOT rush out and buy all of these books in a wild fit of enthusiasm. It is much better to wait until you get to college and see which books are essential to buy and which you can get from the library. When you get to university you can talk to second-year students about which books you will need:

you will probably be able to buy many of them for a fraction of the price from former students or second-hand bookshops. Many universities also have regular book sales. Look out for details on departmental and general notice-boards.

### Stationery

You can buy all your stationery from students' union shops: the prices will be much cheaper than at commercial stationers. However, some commercial stationers do offer student discounts, so keep your eyes peeled for notices advertising this service.

## Choosing and using a bank

The competition for student accounts is very intense. You will be bombarded with freebies at the freshers' fair from banks trying to attract you and prove they are the best. Actually the quality of freebies is probably as good a way as any to make this decision. In reality there is not usually much difference between the facilities banks offer students.

**The things you should consider are:**

☞ whether there are any branches close to your university with cash-point machines

☞ whether they will give you a cheque book and card

☞ how much interest-free overdraft they will offer you and for how long. Some banks pay interest on current accounts and you should find out about the rules which govern this.

It might seem like a long way off, but another thing you should consider is what bank charges are levelled on overdrafts once you graduate and whether they offer preferential rates for graduate loans. Most banks will be more willing to give loans to graduates going into certain fields. If possible, talk to past students about how the bank treated them when they graduated.

I am wary about saying this but I got the impression that the banks were far more lenient with male friends of mine, especially those who were doing science subjects. They always seemed to have less trouble arranging overdrafts and were allowed more money than I was as a humanities female.

*Third-year female student, Wolverhampton University.*

There are good arguments both for and against changing from your home branch. Your decision will depend on where you study and what facilities the local branch has. A branch which is used to dealing with student accounts may be more sympathetic to students' needs but it also might not have the resources to fund many large overdrafts.

It was great when we had the branch on campus but now they have made it a sub-branch of the bank in town. It is much more difficult to get overdrafts now as the town bank manager isn't used to dealing with students.

*Third-year student, Swansea University*

If you have a good record with your bank at home – it helps if your parents also have a good reputation – then it might make sense to stay with that branch. You can usually negotiate overdrafts over the phone and, if you do need to see your manager, then you can arrange to do so in the holidays.

When you set up your account, ask for monthly statements, and when they come check them thoroughly: banks do make mistakes. If you have made a note of every withdrawal – cheque book or cash – and deposit, this should only take a few minutes.

## How to arrange an overdraft

By the December of my first term it was obvious that I'd soon be overdrawn and I felt really despondent. I think that a permanent overdraft facility is a reality of modern student life and the banks do seem to accept this. The difficulties only ever arose when I didn't keep my branch informed. If they knew in advance that a rent cheque was going through, generally speaking they were understanding and appreciated being kept informed. OK, I hated hanging around in bank queues on a regular basis but the end results were far more palatable than the dreaded brown envelope of a bounced cheque. It is honestly so much easier to go and talk it over with a personal banker and have a local branch account.

*Third-year student, Wolverhampton University*

Bank managers are well aware of students' lack of funds but they are also interested in your future earning potential. It is a good idea to tell your bank about any steps you take to improve this, particularly if you are going into a traditionally lucrative profession.

My bank has been great to me, I think because I ring them up at every opportunity with both good news and bad. I have established a good record with them of paying off any debts as soon as I can so they always let me have an extension whenever I ask for it.

*Third-year student, Edinburgh University*

Always contact your bank before you go overdrawn. Banks are not overly impressed with people who just assume they have access to money that is not in their account, and remember: unarranged overdrafts are charged at a higher rate of interest than arranged ones. Write or phone for an appointment. You should be prepared to bargain and ideally have something to offer in return. This can be anything from a vacation job to your next grant cheque, providing it is not too far off.

I got into such a mess in my first year that I had to go to see my bank manager on an extremely regular basis. We are now on first name terms and I always get put through whenever I ring up.

*Second-year student, Edinburgh University*

Make sure you keep a record of how long your overdraft facility lasts and don't automatically assume it will be continued after this date just because you don't have the money to pay it back. You will have to re-negotiate your facility. If you think you need to extend your overdraft, contact your bank well in advance.

I had a student come to me claiming her bank was harassing her by calling at her house. When I looked into this further it turned out that she hadn't opened any of her statements, answered any of their letters or taken any of their phone calls. Once she actually talked to them she was able to sort things out.

*Welfare Officer, Loughborough University*

## Bank charges

Bank charges are the fees that banks take out of your account to cover various transactions such as bounced cheques, letters and interest on overdrafts. They are standard charges but can seem very steep when you have so little money.

My bank wrote to me telling me they couldn't trace an overdraft arrangement on my account and charged me £20 for the privilege, which took me over my long-standing overdraft facility. I was not happy. It is the only time I have ever shouted at someone over the phone. What had happened was that the bank had cancelled my overdraft but not thought to tell me. They re-introduced my overdraft and cancelled the charge.

*Third-year student, University of London*

The best way to avoid bank charges is to arrange everything properly and keep records of all correspondence. Banks are often willing to waive charges if you explain your situation in advance. If you know you are going to go overdrawn, STOP writing cheques and withdrawing money until you have spoken to your bank. You may be able to avoid being charged for going overdrawn, having your cheques bounced and being written to, just by making a phone call or calling in at your branch.

The trouble with debt is that you get into a Catch 22 situation. Once cheques start bouncing you get charged, which takes you even further into debt, so the money isn't there to cover the next cheque and so on. I once got charged £150 in bank charges over two months.

*Third-year student, University of London*

If you find that you have been charged by mistake for something you have arranged in advance then ring at once, making sure you have all the proof you need, and you should get any charges reimbursed.

## Lifesavers ⊗

### Organisations

Department for Education, Sanctuary Buildings, Great Smith Street, London SW1P 3BT. Publications Department, PO Box 2193, London E15 2EU, tel 081-533 2000.

Department for Education for Northern Ireland, Rathgael House, Baloo Road, Bangor, Co Down BT19 7PR, tel 0247 270077.

Scottish Office Education Department, Gyleview House, 3 Redheughs Rigg, South Gyle, Edinburgh EH12 9HH, tel 031-244 5823.

Student Loans Company, 100 Bothwell Street, Glasgow G2 7JD, tel 0345 300900.

Welsh Office Education Department, Companies House, Crown Way, Maindy, Cardiff CF4 3UZ, tel 0222 761456.

### Publications

*A Question of Sponsorship?*, a free leaflet available from the Student Sponsorship Information Services (SSIS), PO Box 36, Newton-Le-Willows, Merseyside WA12 0DW.

*A Year Off... A Year On?* Published for CRAC by Hobsons Publishing PLC.

*Charities Digest*, from the Family Welfare Association, 501–505 Kingsland Road, Dalston, London E8 4AU, tel 071-254 6251. Gives information on charities offering grants to needy students. Cost £14.95.

*Directory of Grant-Making Trusts*, from Charities Aid Foundation, 48 Pembury Road, Tonbridge, Kent TN9 2JD, tel 0732 771333. Gives a list of all grant-making bodies in England and Wales covering all fields of voluntary activities.

Cost £50 + £3.80 postage and packing.

*Money to Study*, published jointly by NUS and the United Kingdom Council for Overseas Student Affairs (UKCOSA). It costs £11.95 and is available from the Educational Grants Advisory Service which is part of the Family Welfare Association. Write to EGAS, c/o Family Welfare Association, 501–505 Kingsland Road, Dalston, London E8 4AU, tel 071-254 6251.

*Sponsorships 1994*, send a cheque or postal order for £3.56 made payable to COIC and send it to Department CW ISCO 5, The Paddock, Frizinghall, Bradford BD9 4HD. Lists employers and professional bodies who offer sponsorship for first degrees, BTEC higher awards and similar courses beginning in 1993.

*Sponsorship and Training Opportunities in Engineering*, free from the Institution of Mechanical Engineers, PO Box 23, Northgate Avenue, Bury St Edmunds IP3⁓ 6BN, tel 0284 763277. Gives details of sponsorships and training offered to sixth-formers and those applying for university places and for final-year students looking for a graduate training post.

*Student Grants and Loans*, a brief guide, available free from the DFE publications department. An easy-to-understand explanation of the application processes behind grants and loans which was given the Crystal Award for plain English. Students in Scotland should get hold of *Student Guides in Scotland – A Guide to Undergraduate Allowances 1994/5* from the Scottish Office. The Welsh Office produces a leaflet on grants and loans in the Welsh language.

*Teacher Training Bursary Scheme* leaflet is available from the TASC Publicity Unit, Elizabeth House, York Road, London SE1 7PH, tel 071-925 6617. Details of bursaries available for PGCE courses in specific shortage subjects. These bursaries are paid on top of regular grant and loan entitlements.

*The Which? Guide to Sponsorship in Higher Education*, from Which?, 2 Marylebone Road, London NW1 4DX and from bookshops.

# 2 Accommodation

## What is available?

When you go to university or college you are not only choosing where you are going to study for the next three or four years, but also where you will be living. It is important to consider carefully what sort of accommodation will suit you. A comfortable home, where you are happy living, will help you study effectively and make the transition into student life much easier.

This chapter will give you tips on how to make this decision, and then how to find the right accommodation. It will tell you about your legal position when you rent from a landlord or landlady, and give you an idea of how much it will cost to live away from home.

## Where to find out

You may be able to choose where you live in the first year. If this is the case then you will be offered a choice of some of the following forms of college accommodation:

☞ a shared or single room in a hall of residence

☞ a room in a shared student house or flat

☞ a place in a student village complex.

You can also choose to rent a house or a flat in the private sector. Wherever you decide to live you will need to apply early to avoid disappointment.

The range of accommodation varies around the country and you should make sure you find out as much about what is available as possible. Start doing this by looking through university prospectuses, although remember that they are there to sell the university's facilities. If the students' union produces an alternative prospectus then this will give you a wider range of accommodation to consider. You should also make sure you look around and ask questions when you visit the university for an open day or interview. If you don't visit the university then you should at least write and ask them specific questions about accommodation.

The students' union tends to be the best place for help, but the accommodation office is another good place to go for information, as it will have details not only about college accommodation but also about the private sector housing available in the area. Many have lists of recommended landlords, landladies, housing associations and agencies. You should contact the accommodation office immediately if you have specific housing needs such as those resulting from a disability or dependants who need to live with you. It is also important that you contact the accommodation office if you are offered a place through clearing. You may not want to accept a clearing place at a university which has no accommodation left and is in a part of the country where it is difficult to rent through the private sector.

## What does it cost?

Your rent will be the largest chunk out of your grant cheque, especially as students are no longer entitled to claim housing benefit. You will need to budget carefully for your rent (see Budgeting in chapter 1), as having nowhere to live, or getting evicted for non-payment, is extremely traumatic and hardly conducive to study. The following table shows a selection of average weekly rents in university towns around the country.

## University accommodation

Unless you have already visited a university, then terms like halls of residence and student flats are unlikely to mean anything to you. This section will tell you about the different forms of accommodation available and help you decide where you will be happiest living.

| | **Accommodatio** | | |
|---|---|---|---|
| | Accommodation in college | | meals provided |
| | self-catered | catered | |
| Birmingham | £22–£31 | £45–£66 | 2 |
| Brighton | £35–£42 | £42–£55 | 2 |
| Bristol | £34–£38 | £53–£70 | 2 weekdays 3 weekends |
| Coventry | £37 | Yes but price not agreed yet | 2 |
| Leeds | £33–£50 | £50–£66 | 2 |
| Leicester | £28 | £53–£70 | 2 weekdays 3 weekends |
| Liverpool | £25–£30 | £52 | 2 |
| London | £50 | £75 | Varies according individual college contact them for details |
| Loughborough | £28 | £53–£70 | 2 |
| Manchester | £27 | £57 | 2 weekdays 3 weekends |
| Reading | £34–£47 | £73–£60 | 2 weekdays 3 weekends |
| York | £23–£28 | – | – |

## ross the UK

| of 1st years in halls | guaranteed place for 1st years? | holiday accommodation? | private rented accommodation |
|---|---|---|---|
| 80% | Yes, if 1st choice and apply before 31 May | No | £25–£35 |
| 60% | No | Yes | £40–£45 |
| 80% | Yes to under-21s if you apply by 31 May | Yes | £38 |
| 75% | Yes, not necessarily in halls | Yes | £25–£35 |
| 95% | Yes | Can be arranged | £33 |
| 75% | Yes | No | £28 |
| 75% | Yes, if 1st choice | Yes | £30 |
| 70% | Yes in some colleges | Yes in some colleges | £55–£70 according to which zone you live in |
| 65% | Yes, if you apply early | No | £30 |
| 90% | Yes | Yes | £30–£35 |
| 95% | Yes if you apply by end of May | Yes | £35–£40 |
| 96% | Yes | Possible | £35–£40 |

| | **Accommodatio** | | |
| | Accommodation in college | | meals provided |
| | self-catered | catered | |
| Aberdeen | £38 | £52 | 2 |
| Dundee | £30–£35 | £53 | 2 |
| Edinburgh | £38 | £60 | 2 weekdays 1 weekend |
| Aberystwyth | £44 | £38–£41 | 2 |
| Cardiff | £27–£41 | £51–£53 | 2 |
| Swansea | £22–£31 | £42–£59 | 2 |
| Belfast | £26–£30 | £45–£51 | 2 |
| Coleraine | £20–£31 | £20–£31 | Not included in re |

The figures shown are from 1

## ross the UK

| of 1st years in halls | guaranteed place for 1st years? | holiday accommodation? | private rented accommodation |
|---|---|---|---|
| 80% | Yes | No | £31 |
| 85% | Yes | No | £28–£32 |
| 85% | Yes | Yes | £38 |
| 95% same hall | Yes | Yes not always | £35–£40 |
| 85% | Yes | Yes | £20–£40 |
| 95% | No | No | £30 |
| 80% | No | Yes | £20–£25 |
| 70% | Sometimes | Depends | £22–£25 |

table is meant to be a comparative guide.

## Halls of residence

> I have lived in halls for four years. It is mainly because my warden is such a lovely lady that I have been very happy there. I would definitely recommend all first years to go into a hall of residence as it is the best way to make friends. I am still in contact with the friends I made in my first hall.

*Welfare Officer, Loughborough University*

'Hall of residence' describes a vast spectrum of buildings. You could end up living in a huge concrete tower block or in an old building overlooking a pretty courtyard. Most, however, are purpose-built with single study bedrooms, although some have double bedrooms so you might end up sharing a room. This may sound like a frightening prospect, but some people find that it works well and it will certainly reduce your rent.

> Sharing a room is decidedly not for the ham-handed. My room-mate has a very beautiful suede jacket, which came to grief one night when in my clumsiness I tipped a wax candle down it. Nearly the end of a beautiful friendship.

*Second-year student, Durham University*

A single study bedroom in a hall of residence will be pretty much the same everywhere. You will be provided with a bed, a desk, a chair, some shelves and somewhere to store your clothes. There are obviously variations and additions to this theme, such as a sink and more floor space, but these are the basics you can expect.

*This map shows the locations referred to on the accommodation table.*

My college has a huge variety of halls. Some are old and very pretty buildings and others are not. Unfortunately we don't get a choice of where we want to live. I have ended up in this horrible 1970s brick building where the only difference between one set of rooms and another is the variety of revolting-coloured industrial paint the doors are decorated with. It could be worse, I could have ended up in one of the pea green rooms.

*Third-year student, University of London*

Some universities will also be able to offer you a choice of whether you want to live in a single-sex or a mixed hall. Single-sex halls are usually for women only. There will probably be a time limit by which all guests have to be out but, other than that, it will be run in the same way as other halls of residence. Most mixed halls will also be segregated to some extent. This is normally done by placing women on one corridor and men on another, although usually you will all live on the same floor.

Halls offer full board (where all your meals are provided), part board (where some of your meals are provided) or self-catering accommodation. Student flats, sometimes called halls, are described on page 55.

### What it is like to live in a hall of residence?

I love living in halls because life is so easy. You have people who come in and clean for you and cook your food.

*President of the Guild of Students, Aberystwyth University*

Living in a hall of residence can be a lot of fun if you enjoy meeting and mixing with people, and has advantages even if you find this difficult. The obvious advantage of living in hall is that you do not need to worry about bills, cleaning, landlords, plumbing, or even – in catered halls – about food. In addition, halls are usually near to the university and students' union which makes it much easier to get involved with all student activities. Most universities give priority to first-year students and some even allocate all rooms exclusively to freshers. This means there is a very strong feeling that everyone is in the same boat, which can be a great comfort.

I had a great time in the first few weeks because I was living in a small hall. We spent our first weeks going round in a large group which meant it was really easy to go up and talk to loads of people.

*Third-year student, Edinburgh University*

However, as with any accommodation, there are also disadvantages. You may not like the people you are living with. Do not panic if this happens to you, particularly in the first few weeks. There is inevitably a period of adjustment while a group of people gets used to living with each other and away from home. If you are still unhappy later in the first term then you can go to your warden and request a transfer to a different hall. You will usually find wardens and accommodation officers are sympathetic to your problems and will do their best to arrange a transfer if a room is available elsewhere.

Noise can be a problem. After the initial jollity of freshers' week it can be really annoying if your neighbours insist on staying up all night and playing student pranks when you have to get up for a 9 am lecture. You should put a complaint in to the warden if you are regularly being disturbed by noisy neighbours and antisocial behaviour.

## Facilities in halls

You should definitely check the facilities various halls of residence offer. Many larger halls have their own bar and even sports facilities, and are completely self-contained social and living centres. This could be important if the hall is a long way from the university. On the other hand, you may not want to live with such a large crowd of people and may be prepared to put up with a couple of gas rings and a half-mile walk to the nearest washing machine because you prefer to live in a smaller group. The checklist on page 54 shows the facilities you can expect to find in a hall. Decide which are important to you and check which hall offers them in your chosen university.

## Food in halls

It is particularly important to check out all hall catering facilities. Self-catering options will be cheaper in terms of your rent but the practical problems might outweigh the savings. You may have to fight for cooker space with ten other people who all want to eat at the same time. There can also be a problem with storing food. Most hall rooms are not designed to house a week's rations as well as you, your books and clothes. Food stored in public places has a nasty habit of vanishing, especially as term draws to a close and grant cheques dwindle. This is why so many halls of residence have a preponderance of plastic bags hanging from the windows. They are acting as improvised larders for students who have got fed up with finding that the milk for their essential morning cup of coffee has disappeared overnight.

Shared kitchen and cooking facilities can also become really disgusting after a whole corridor of students has tried to cook its evening meal at the same time. After a few weeks you will find that the person who has a massive fry-up for breakfast every morning and never washes up afterwards really gets on your nerves. It is definitely worth complaining if one individual is responsible for turning the communal kitchen into a pig sty, especially as you will have the support of your fellow kitchen users. It is more difficult, however, if there are several people to blame. It is worth bringing it up though, before tempers get too frayed.

You may decide that eating hall meals is a better option. You will probably be given breakfast and dinner but may have to buy your own lunch. You will be restricted by meal times, which can be a pain if you take part in lots of activities or the dining hall is far away from your department or hall. It is also not very convenient if you find it difficult to get up in the mornings.

If you are vegetarian it is particularly important that you make sure there is such a thing as a vegetarian alternative and that the choice is varied.

I am a bit fed up with the frequency of being given baked beans and chips as a vegetarian. If I see another stuffed pepper I will scream.

*Welfare Officer, Liverpool University*

It might sound obvious, but a healthy body is very important to a healthy mind. A significant number of students suffer from mild malnutrition, so make sure you budget adequately for food and choose the catering option which best suits you.

### How halls are run

There will be hall rules which you have to follow. These are usually designed to make sure particularly antisocial behaviour, such as constant noise, is not allowed to run riot and that the rest of the residents are protected.

Our hall rules say that more than four people in a room constitutes a party.

*President of the Students' Association, Edinburgh University*

You will usually have to get permission to hold a party and may have to make special arrangements if you want a friend to stay. The rules governing behaviour that does not affect the other residents are not usually as rigorously enforced, although some institutions do still have tales of boyfriends and girlfriends having to flee across the grounds via the nearest window. Make sure you know what the rules are: it can save a lot of unnecessary arguments between you and your warden.

I remember one particularly cold night when my warden told us that, although hall rules said that beds shouldn't be shared, this was one night when she would positively recommend at least two in a bed.

*Welfare Officer, Loughborough University*

The warden, often an academic postgraduate student, usually lives in the hall of residence, and is responsible for the administration. Your warden is the first point of contact in an emergency or if you have any questions or complaints about the hall you are living in. Some larger halls may also have committees. These will include student representatives who will be included in the discussion of plans for any development work, decoration, policy and budgetary decisions.

Your warden or your hall rep is unlikely to be the first official person you meet, though. This is will probably be your cleaner, usually at a very unsociable hour the morning after you have celebrated your arrival. Cleaners have keys to your room and will want to hoover and clean thoroughly at least once a week. It is a very good idea to co-operate fully with your cleaners as they can become very important allies. If you do not want to be disturbed first thing in the morning, then find out what code operates in your hall. It may involve leaving a note on your door or leaving your bin outside.

**What happens in the holidays?**

Something you should consider when thinking about living in a hall of residence is what you are going to do in the vacations. Some halls will expect you to move out and clear your room a day or two after term finishes. This is not a problem if you have parents prepared to act as chauffeurs at the end of each term or live in halls where

secure storage is available for those belongings you don't fancy lugging back on the train. For those who have nowhere to go in the holidays or who want to stay in the area, it may be possible to arrange holiday accommodation with the college. Some colleges, for instance, run schemes whereby students are given accommodation and spending money in return for office or maintenance work. If you do need to stay, make sure you ask about what provisions there are.

Our university employs students over the vacation period in the office helping to get things organised for the arrival of freshers. However, we can't offer that many jobs and it is not something students should rely on as secure holiday employment.

*Welfare Officer, a university in the North East*

### Availability of rooms in halls

The availability of rooms in halls of residence is very varied in different institutions. Even those universities that used to be able to house a good proportion of their students in halls are now finding it more difficult as student numbers have increased dramatically in the last three years. Priority does tend to be given to first years, but you should still apply as early as possible if this type of accommodation appeals to you.

### Hall fees

You will owe your hall fees to the university. If you still have outstanding debts by the time you come to graduate you will not be given your degree results until you have cleared them. Each university has its own criteria about when hall fees should be paid. If you get the option then you should pay your hall fees as soon as you arrive. Once you have met the biggest single expenditure you have, it is easier to see what you have left to live on.

### What happens if it all goes wrong?

I was told that accommodation was guaranteed to all first-year students. What this actually meant was that hall places were given out on a first come first served basis and the rest were given a list of local bed and breakfasts. This list was given to all first years

in this predicament at all four colleges in
Edinburgh which meant there were no
vacancies. I eventually found a B and B to
share with a friend of mine. I understand the
university realised they made a mistake that
year.

*Second-year student, Edinburgh University*

Every year you will hear horror stories of new students
having to sleep on gym floors or even having soup runs
set up to feed them. There are occasions when administrative errors or building schedules gone awry mean that
there are too many students for too few rooms, but these
are the exception, not the rule.

It is really important that you take with you copies of
all the paperwork you have had from the university about
accommodation. If you are one of those unfortunate
people who ends up with no accommodation, take any
documentation you have to the accommodation office
and to the students' union. They will be doing their best
to help you find suitable accommodation. The important
thing is not to panic and to follow the advice you are
given. You will probably be given a list of emergency
accommodation facilities in the area (see Emergency
Housing page 81) which should give you enough breath-
ing space to get something permanent sorted out. If you
do not feel the university is doing enough to help you
then take your complaints to the students' union.

When I came back in the second year I was
given somewhere to live 40 miles away and
Wales is not exactly famous for its public
transport provision, so I turned it down. I
had to sleep outdoors for the first weekend.

*Third-year student, Lampeter University*

**Questions to ask when viewing halls of residence**

❏ What is the variety of accommodation offered?

❏ How much choice will I have over where I live?

❏ Can I choose to live in a single-sex or a mixed hall?

❏ Will I have to share a room?

❏ Could I stay over any of the vacation periods?

❏ How many students does the hall house?

❏ How is the hall heated?

❏ What are the fees?

❏ Do the hall fees include catering?

❏ What are the catering facilities like?

❏ What are the rooms like – what furniture do they have?

❏ What social/washing/cleaning facilities are offered?

❏ Is there a bar?

❏ Is there a sports hall?

❏ Is there a TV room/common room?

❏ How many people have to share the bathroom/ shower/kitchen facilities?

❏ How far away is the hall from public transport?

❏ How frequent is public transport, and what is the cost?

❏ How far is it from the university/relevant department?

❏ Who are the other residents – first years, third years, postgraduates?

❏ Is there parking space?

❏ Could I store a bike?

❏ Can I leave things in my room/store things during the vacation?

## Other forms of college accommodation

Some universities have been quite entrepreneurial in the alternatives they offer their students and have bought hotels or taken over buildings which they manage as co-ops. If you study at a large university then you will probably find quite a range of college accommodation. It is worth taking time to find out what is on offer, particularly as these alternatives are increasingly being offered to first years owing to the shortage of places in halls. Ask your accommodation office for details.

## Student houses and flats

It is quite common for universities to have purpose-built self-catering houses and flats for groups of their students. They might require you to meet certain criteria but it can be an excellent way of combining independence with the security of renting from the university.

As in a hall, you will probably live in your own room with a bed, desk, cupboard and so on, and there will also be a kitchen, bathroom and maybe a living room, shared by all the residents of the flat or house. There may or may not be a warden, but if there is one, then he or she is likely to take a lower profile than a hall warden.

The only problem with our student flats is that they all look the same. It is quite difficult to decide where you are, especially disconcerting when you wake up the morning after a party. A friend of mine made the classic mistake of walking into what he thought was his girlfriend's room only to find he was in the wrong flat.

*Fourth-year student, Edinburgh University*

The disadvantage of this form of accommodation is that – as in a hall – you will not get any choice about who you share with in the first year. This can be more of a problem in a smaller flat or house than in a larger hall of residence. If you really can't stand your flatmates then go to the accommodation office and request a transfer.

## Student villages

Student villages are collections of houses owned by the university and leased to its students. Increasingly universities are providing this type of accommodation. The houses are shared by about seven to ten students who all have their own room but who share a communal kitchen and bathroom. They do not have live-in wardens so, if you are a confident person who wants to make many friends, this type of accommodation is a good option.

When I moved into my village we had no electricity for the first few days. This was a bit of a disaster as nobody's alarm clock went off so we all missed registration and the principal's speech. The water had also gone off the day before 17,000 students were due to move in. It was a bit of a nightmare but, once the initial teething problems were sorted out, it became a great place to live. I have my independence and am surrounded by other students.

*First-year student, Swansea University*

Many student villages were originally intended to house second- and third-year students but, because of the recent increase in first-year applicants, they are now being offered to freshers. Details will be available from the university accommodation office.

### Questions to ask about student flats, houses and villages

- ❏ How are people selected to share a flat/house?
- ❏ How far away is the university/relevant department?
- ❏ How many students live in the flat/house?
- ❏ How many kitchens and bathrooms do we have to share?
- ❏ What is in each room?
- ❏ Can I stay over the vacation periods?
- ❏ What are the fees and when do I have to pay them?
- ❏ Is there a warden?
- ❏ Who do I contact with any complaints or queries?
- ❏ Who is responsible for the maintenance?

LIBRARY
BISHOP BURTON COLLE
BEVERLEY HU17 8QG

- ❏ Are the residents responsible for keeping the flat/house clean?

- ❏ Will I have to bring my own cooking things, cutlery and crockery?

- ❏ Is there a washing machine?

- ❏ How far away are the local food shops/markets?

- ❏ How far away is the local public transport?

- ❏ How frequently does the local transport run?

- ❏ How much does transport cost?

- ❏ Is there parking?

- ❏ Could I store a bike here?

## Leased properties

In my first year I lived in a single-sex hall of residence where all guests had to be out by 10.30 pm but we all ignored that. In my second and third years I lived in a house leased through the college but we dealt directly with the landlord. This was a great way of having both independence and security.

*Third-year student, University of London*

Many universities operate schemes whereby they rent local properties which they then sub-let to students. There are sometimes certain requirements you have to fulfil, such as being a second- or final-year student, before you are eligible to rent a house or a flat through the college.

Some universities also rent short-lease properties. These are flats and houses which cannot be leased for long periods of time. They will usually be very cheap but there is a real danger that you will be evicted with very little notice.

I lived in a short-lease property rented by the college. It was a brilliant way of renting an extremely cheap flat right in the centre of London and turned most of my friends green with jealousy. However, they weren't quite so jealous when I had to leave a few weeks before my finals because the building was being pulled down.

*Third-year student, University of London*

### Questions to ask about leased properties

❏ Can I choose who I share with?

❏ How far away is the university/relevant department?

❏ Will I deal with the university or the landlord/landlady?

❏ Do I have the same rights as any other private tenant?

❏ Who do I go to with complaints or queries?

❏ How much notice will I be given before being evicted?

❏ How do I pay my rent and when?

❏ Do I have to pay a deposit: if so, can I have a signed receipt?

❏ Will I have to arrange to have the utilities connected?

❏ Will the bills be in my name?

❏ Who is responsible for repairs?

❏ What security provisions are there?

❏ What are the kitchen/bathroom facilities like?

❏ How much of the furniture is staying?

❏   How far away are the local food shops/markets?

❏   How far away is the nearest public transport?

❏   How frequently does the public transport run?

❏   What is the cost of public transport?

## The private sector

After a while you will become very familiar with the term 'student housing'. This is used to refer to a property in poor repair, usually one that isn't particularly tidy and is shared by more people than it was originally intended to house. Students cannot afford to rent palatial mansions. It is remarkable how quickly you adjust to living in this sort of accommodation, mainly because all your friends are living in the same conditions. It can, however, be a bit of a shock for visiting parents who have not had previous experience of student housing. You should just be careful that you do not end up renting a house which is very much sub-standard as you could land yourself with a whole load of problems.

You will have to decide what sort of private accommodation you want to rent and where you want to live. You can share a house or a flat with other students or friends, live by yourself in a bedsit, or live in the same property as your landlord or landlady as a lodger. You may want to live in an area with lots of other students or prefer life outside 'student ghetto land'. There are advantages and disadvantages with every option: the table at the end of this chapter should help you make your decision.

Looking for a room, flat or house to rent can seem like a daunting task, but providing you plan well and seek as much help and advice as you feel you need, it should be very exciting and give you a great sense of freedom.

### Beginning the search

You should start looking for somewhere to live well before term starts. You have enough to do at the beginning of term without worrying about where you are going to live and who you are going to share with.

Go to your accommodation office and ask for a list of landlords and landladies who rent to students in the area. They should also be able to give you a list of reputable housing associations and agencies. Agencies will charge you a fee of two weeks' rent or more if you lease a property through them, so make sure you budget for it when exploring this avenue. They also often charge for the holidays, even if you haven't yet moved in. They won't, however, charge you for supplying a list of properties.

Your students' union will also have information on available properties, particularly if it has an accommodation notice-board or student newspaper that carries advertisements. In addition, you can look through the classified columns of local newspapers or use word of mouth if you already know people in the area.

It is a good idea to try to take over a house from another group of students as you will be able to talk to them about the problems they have had during the year and their relationship with the property owner or agent. Ideally, you should always talk to any previous tenants. Forewarned can definitely be forearmed when it comes to dealing with property owners and building matters.

## Viewing a property

It is a good idea to go and look at lots of properties before renting to see what is available, but you will need to get in quickly when you spot a good one. You should definitely go and see a property before renting it. Women should, if possible, take someone with them for security reasons. If this is not possible let someone know where you are going and arrange to see the flat during the daytime.

### Security

Look at how secure the property is. Ideally the front door should have at least two locks on it, a Yale and a deadlock spaced apart from each other by about 30 cm. If there is a communal entrance then look at the locks on this as well and find out who has keys to it.

### Fire escapes

You should ask the owner whether there are any fire escapes. Some owners are not good at meeting the legal requirements. The local health and safety department will be able to tell you what the minimum fire precautions should be for the property you want to rent. If the landlord or landlady has not taken these precautions into account, then you should ask for it to be done before you move in.

## Neighbours

I think it is a really good idea to make friends with your neighbours. I had a party in my flat. It wasn't a particularly outrageous party and I did invite the neighbours. They didn't come, but they didn't complain either.

*President of the Students' Association, Edinburgh University*

It might seem like a good idea to live next door to the best pub in the area, but you may not think so after you have been woken up every night at closing time. It is worth looking out for potentially noisy neighbours, residential or commercial.

Don't ever live opposite Finchley Central station. My regular alarm call at 7 am each day is London Underground's announcement of delays on the Northern Line.

*Second-year student, University of London*

### Heating

Most students will be choosing flats and houses during the summer months, so remember that a nice bright, sunny day can make a big difference to the way something looks. You should check what form of heating the property has and ask about how much it costs and if it is included in your rent. Gas and electricity companies have saver schemes which can be a good way of cutting the cost of heating the property.

High-ceilinged, big-windowed Victorian houses may look attractive but they are very expensive to heat. If you live in a terraced block surrounded on either side by neighbours who are not students, then they will probably heat their houses better and you will benefit.

You should definitely rent a property where you have control over the heating: you might just want to wear lots of extra sweaters during the winter months rather than have huge heating bills. Whatever you do, do not heat a property using electric fan heaters as these only give off very localised heat and are extremely expensive to run.

## Gas appliances

It is REALLY IMPORTANT that you check all gas appliances, as you cannot smell the poisonous carbon monoxide that faulty appliances give out. In 1992 Clare Watkinson, a student at Aston University, died because of a faulty gas heater. There are, however, some basic warning signs you can look for and if you feel listless, lack energy and get 'flu-like' symptoms when you are around gas then turn the appliance off and get it checked immediately. You should look for any signs of staining, discolouration or sooting around appliances as these can all be danger signs. Look in the local phone book for your nearest CORGI-registered installer or British Gas office and ask for your appliances to be checked. When viewing a property with gas appliances ask the landlord when they were last checked. If they haven't been serviced for more than 12 months then ask for this to be done before you agree to move in.

## Structure

Check for signs of damp and rot. These are not as easy to spot on a summer's day as in mid-winter. Tide marks on the ceiling, walls or floor or recently-decorated patches are good indicators of these problems. You may decide to rent a house with signs of damp anyway. If you do, then you should make sure the damp is not so extensive that it is going to cause regular problems which will mean you are constantly having to ask the landlord to repair collapsing walls. You should also make sure any signs of damp are listed on the inventory (see Deposits on page 66).

You should turn on all the taps to make sure they work

and look closely at the loo to check it works and is not leaking.

Take a look at the outside of the property. Some signs of damage are not always visible but if there are tiles missing from the roof or water marks around the guttering then it is not likely to be the most structurally sound house.

**Furniture**
See whether the house has enough furniture in it for all the residents and that it is in adequate condition. You need a bed, desk, chair, shelves and space to store your clothes. If the house has more furniture than you think you will need then ask the owner to store it for you. Do not try to cram it all into a damp attic as this will ruin the furniture and the damage will be taken out of your deposit. If you look around a house that is still occupied, check which furniture belongs to the current occupants and which will be left behind.

You will sometimes find unfurnished properties on the market. The rent will be cheaper but you will have to make sure you and your friends have enough furniture for the whole property and that it is available for when you want to move in. It is no good relying on Aunt Gladys's sofa if she can't give it to you for six months.

**The kitchen**
Inspect the fridge and the cooker to check that they work. You should also look at the space available for preparing food and remember that all your house- or flatmates might want to cook at the same time. The other thing to consider is how many power points there are in the kitchen and, again, bear in mind the number of people who might want to use the kitchen. There is nothing more annoying than having to unplug the kettle every time someone wants to iron a shirt. As with the furniture, check what equipment belongs to the house and what to the occupants. Large kitchens are extremely useful in shared households.

**Transport**

This is a very important factor to consider, particularly for women. Look carefully at what is available in the area and imagine yourself travelling back late at night alone. If possible take a look at the house at night so you can see whether the street lighting is adequate.

You should ask how much public transport costs, and how frequently it runs to and from town and university. You will also need to know how late the transport runs at night. If you rely on your own car or bike then you should look at parking and storage facilities.

**Deposits**

A deposit is usually one month's rent and is paid in advance to cover the property owner against any loss or damage. This means that before you are able to move in you will have to have enough money to cover the deposit and a month's rent. Because rented property is not usually on the market for very long you might want to carry your cheque book around with you when looking at houses so you have the option of putting down a deposit as soon as you find one you like. But beware of making a snap judgment under pressure that you might regret later.

Your deposit will be returned to you at the end of your contract providing the property is in the same condition as it was when you moved in. The landlord or landlady will measure this against an inventory of contents and the general condition. You should make sure that you agree with everything written down on the inventory when you move in and, if the property is already damaged in any way, have it included on the list.

Make sure you get a written, signed receipt for your deposit and do not lose it during the year. Cover yourself by taking several photocopies, as a month's rent is extremely useful at the end of a year of surviving on a student grant.

If your landlord or landlady refuses to give you back your deposit you should wait seven days after your contract finishes and then write asking for either your money back or a detailed letter stating the reasons why they will not return it to you. If you are not satisfied with the reply then take it to your students' union or your local Citizens' Advice Bureau for advice.

### Renting in England, Wales and Northern Ireland

The advantage of the 1988 Housing Act for students is that it is now possible for property owners to rent for academic years rather than calendar years. However, it also means that there is no such thing as a market rent and so you have little protection from people wanting to charge you extortionate rents for substandard properties.

### Tenancy agreements

I found that some landlords wouldn't rent to me when they found out I was doing law. It probably meant they were trying to get us to sign a particularly dodgy agreement.

*Third-year student, Wolverhampton University*

Tenancy agreements can appear to be very frightening documents. The basic rule of thumb is not to sign anything that you are not happy with or do not understand. If you have any questions then you should take your contract to your students' union or the local Citizens' Advice Bureau. You will usually be offered one of two types of tenancy agreement: an assured tenancy or an assured shorthold tenancy. It is a good idea to find out the name of your landlord or landlady, even if you rent through an agency, just in case.

### Assured tenancies

An assured tenancy lasts for an indefinite period of time and your rent cannot be increased during the first 12 months. After that the owner can increase the rent but if you feel it is too high for the area you are living in you can appeal to your local rent assessment committee (see Lifesavers at the end of this chapter).

**Assured shorthold tenancies**

An assured shorthold tenancy is very similar to an assured tenancy except that it is for a fixed term, usually six months or a year. It is the most common form of tenancy and gives you the same rights as an assured tenancy. Owners who are used to renting to students will often allow you to sign a contract for the academic year so that you don't have the expense of renting over the summer holidays.

You must look carefully at the tenancy agreement to see who is responsible for the rent. In shared houses you will usually be offered a joint tenancy. You must put all the tenants' names on the contract so you are all jointly liable.

You should also find out who is responsible for getting co-tenants. One of your flatmates may want to leave early and you might not like the idea of a complete stranger moving in. Usually the owner will be happy to let you arrange your co-tenants, but check the small print in your agreement.

If you do want to leave early then you will have to give the landlord as much notice as the interval between rent payments: if you pay rent monthly then you will have to give a month's notice. If you don't do this you will forfeit your deposit. You may, however, be able to come to an arrangement with your landlord or landlady if you find someone to take your place.

**Licences**

What tends to happen in Wolverhampton is that there are a number of families who own multiple properties in the family name. Because they don't want to declare the rent they get as business income, there are a lot of licence agreements around, which are much cheaper than the market rent for the area.

*Third-year student, Wolverhampton University*

If you live with your landlord or landlady you will normally sign a licence agreement. Lodgers, live-in helpers and people who rent the spare room to help with the mortgage are all given a licence contract. A licence agreement merely gives you the right to be in the property, not to RESIDE in it. This means that you do not have the same legal protection as people who have signed a tenancy agreement. You won't, for instance, have any protection against eviction. However, you might want to consider signing a licence agreement if it means you are able to rent a cheap property. If you do decide to accept a licence then show it to your students' union or Citizens' Advice Bureau office before signing.

### Protection from eviction

Under an assured tenancy the landlord can give you two months' notice to leave if, for example, he wants the property back or if he has defaulted on the mortgage and the building is being repossessed. You can also be forced to leave with two weeks' notice if you haven't paid your rent for three months. These are termed mandatory grounds. There are also reasons known as discretionary grounds for which you can be asked to leave within two weeks. These will be enforced if you are consistently late in paying your rent, if the property has deteriorated due to your negligence or if you have damaged the furniture. You have the same rights under an assured shorthold tenancy.

Under a licence agreement you have no protection from eviction and your landlord can turn you out at any time without notice.

Before you can be evicted under an assured tenancy agreement you must be served with a Notice to Quit after which the courts have to grant a Possession Order. The grounds for granting a Possession Order vary, so you should seek advice immediately if you are threatened with eviction. The 1988 Housing Act gives you protection from illegal eviction. If you feel your landlord has used unreasonable force, or harassed you into leaving, you can take him to court and claim part of the profit he has made by forcing you to leave.

**Rent**

There are a number of ways in which you may be asked to pay your rent. Many property owners will want you to set up a standing order at the bank which your parents may be asked to guarantee. If this is likely to be a problem then you should find out about how you will be required to pay your rent before you sign any contracts.

If your landlord or landlady asks for a series of post-dated cheques to cover your rent offer to pay by standing order instead. It can be difficult to cancel cheques at a later date if things go wrong. Make sure you keep your own record of your rent payments just in case there are any problems later.

> We had an on-going battle with our landlord because he wouldn't carry out the repairs so we ended up owing three months' rent. We got a letter from his solicitor and wrote back saying, 'no repairs, no rent'. We didn't hear anything from him after that.

*Second-year student, University of London*

As the fair rent agreement has now been abolished, there is no legal protection for tenants who feel they are being charged too much. You should look in the local paper to get an idea of the rents for comparable properties before signing a contract.

## Renting in Scotland

Most houses in Scotland are let under an assured tenancy agreement which gives the tenant certain rights. However, there are lettings which are not assured tenancies, the main ones which affect students being those where you sub-let a house from the university or live as a lodger.

### Tenancy agreements

There must be some form of tenancy agreement between you and your landlord or landlady and it should cover the length of the tenancy, how and when the rent will be paid, how much rent will be paid, who is responsible for the internal and external maintenance of the property and any restriction on the use of the property. These have to be agreed by both the landlord and the tenant under a contractual assured tenancy agreement. If you do not agree with the terms a property owner offers you under a statutory assured tenancy agreement then you can apply to a Rent Assessment Committee which will act as a mediator. The terms it decides will become legally binding.

There are two types of tenancy agreement in Scotland: a short assured tenancy, which must last for at least six months, and an assured tenancy. You will initially be given a contractual assured tenancy. This will last for a set period of time after which your landlord or landlady will serve you with a Notice to Quit. If you want to remain in the property then you and the property owner can negotiate a statutory assured tenancy under which you will have different rights. It is important to be clear about which type you are signing.

**Protection from eviction**
Before a landlord or landlady can evict you, you must be served with a Notice to Quit, followed by a Notice of Proceedings indicating that they are taking proceedings to regain possession, and finally they must obtain an Order for Possession from the sheriff of the local court. It is a criminal offence for you to be turned out of your home without a Court Order or if your landlord or landlady has been using threatening tactics, violence or withholding services. If you experience any harassment then you should contact the police immediately.

There are specific criteria which a Notice to Quit must fulfil and if you are served with one before the end of your agreed contract you should contact your students' association, your local District Housing Department or Citizens' Advice Bureau for advice.

**Rent**
The amount of rent you are charged should be a market rent. This is simply the amount of rent a tenant and landlord agree is reasonable, taking into account the property's location and condition. If you cannot agree on

a market rent then you can apply to the independent Rent Assessment Committee for arbitration. You should also make sure that both you and your landlord or landlady agree on when the rent should be paid and how. If you are renting on a weekly basis the owner must supply you with a rent book.

You can be asked for a returnable deposit of up to two months' rent as a protection against any damage but it is illegal for you to be charged a premium, or 'key money', before you move in. You can be asked to pay for the furniture and fittings as part of the tenancy agreement.

However, you must be given an itemised list of all the pieces of furniture and the prices. Anyone charging an unreasonably high price for furniture can be prosecuted.

Anyone renting in Scotland, particularly if they are not familiar with Scottish law, should get hold of a copy of *Assured tenancies in Scotland – Your Rights and Responsibilities* which is available from the Scottish Office Environmental Department, St Andrews House, Edinburgh EH11 3DG (tel: 031-244 2407). You should also contact the student advice centre at your university for specific advice on renting local properties.

### Who to share with

Many students choose to live in a shared house with a group of other students or friends. When this works well it is a great way to live but even the best of friendships can crumble under arguments about whose turn it is to do the washing up or who used the last of the milk. It is a good idea to draw up a set of house rules like this one and agree on a complaints procedure right at the start to try to avoid arguments later.

The key to sharing with other people is flexibility. In a family situation the roles in a household are often clearly defined. When you move in with a group of peers then you have to define the rules around everyone's needs. The best house- or flatmates are people who are flexible and have

## Rules of the house

- Last one out and last one in at night locks up and checks all windows.
- All phone calls must be logged in the book (be honest!).
- No loud music after midnight (unless everyone is invited to the party).
- **Always** clean the bath after using it (rugby players take note).
- Keep the communal areas tidy (your mum doesn't live here).
- Washing up left on the sink for more than two days will be dumped on your bed.
- Food and drink not labelled with your name will be regarded as communal (you have been warned).
- Household chores (yes we all have to do our bit) are allocated according to the rota.
- No smoking except in your room.

the same sense of space as you. It is no good sharing with someone who always wants to arrange house outings if you are someone who wants to come back and flop in front of the TV every night.

The ideal co-tenants are not necessarily your best friends. It is very easy to reach the end of the first year with ten people you regard as good friends and decide it would be really nice if you all moved in together. It is a much better idea to split into two or three households. Living with people can be stressful and you shouldn't put all your eggs into one basket and live in the same house with all your friends. You will need somewhere to escape to at times, to give you and your co-tenants some space.

You also need to look at how compatible you are with the people you are going to live with and, again, this doesn't always mean being good friends. Your best friend might have a horrible boyfriend or girlfriend or be fanatically tidy. They might be really messy in the kitchen or hopeless with money. These are all things which won't necessarily make them a bad friend but might well make them difficult to share a house with.

A first-year student whom none of us knew beforehand moved into our house after one of our flatmates had to move out. Within a week her friends had thrown up all over the place, things had gone missing from our rooms and she had incited several near fights. The final straw came when I stepped into the shower only to come ankle deep in fag butts and ash. At which point I confronted her and ever since then we haven't had any problems, in fact she's been really quiet.

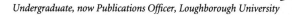

*Undergraduate, now Publications Officer, Loughborough University*

You might decide that you are the sort of person who is better suited to living by yourself. Renting a bedsit is the best way to do this on a student grant. It can bring a wonderful sense of freedom and you may really appreciate being able to relax in your own home. However, it can also be quite lonely, particularly for a woman: your social life may be restricted because of the dangers of travelling back late at night by yourself.

Another major decision you might have to make is whether or not you should move in with your boyfriend or girlfriend. You will have to be very sure of your relationship before you take this step: remember that student relationships are often exploratory and definitely subject to the stresses of academic pressure. It is traumatic if you have to move out of your home at any point but, if this move is coupled with the emotional distress of a broken relationship, it is a particularly difficult situation to cope with. If this coincides with exam time your performance will suffer. On the other hand, living with a partner in a strong relationship can help you both handle the pressures of student life and exams.

There is more advice on the practicalities of sharing in chapter 3.

## Landlords and landladies

When you sign a tenancy agreement you are entering into a legal contract with your landlord or landlady under which you both have to fulfil certain obligations. It is illegal, for example, for them to discriminate against you on racial or sexual grounds. If you feel you have suffered in this way then you should go to your students' union or local Citizens' Advice Bureau for advice on the procedures to follow.

I came back to find that the landlord had changed the locks on the door. I went to the local police station to tell them what had happened. They just told me how to break in and then left me to it. I had had a long-standing argument with my landlord but I was a tad surprised at the attitude of the police.

*Second-year student, University of London*

Landlords do have the right to enter their properties to inspect them or carry out repairs but they must give you reasonable notice. This is usually 24 hours and, if your landlord contravenes this on a regular basis, it can be regarded as harassment. You should get help from a local housing advice centre or the tenancy relations officer at your local authority if this happens to you.

The landlord also has responsibility for the structure, sanitation and plumbing of the property you are renting.

This means that any repairs which need to be done in these areas are his or her responsibility. If you feel your landlord is not fulfilling this requirement or is being slow to act then you should contact the Environmental Health Department of the local authority.

## Paying bills

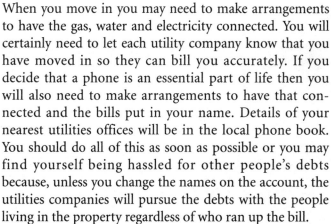

You can get lots of hassles with finalising bills. The people in the flat before us had rung up BT and asked for a final bill, which BT had interpreted as meaning we wanted the phone disconnected. They then tried to charge us a reconnection fee. Apparently what you have to ask for is a meter reading.

*Fourth-year student, Edinburgh University*

When you move in you may need to make arrangements to have the gas, water and electricity connected. You will certainly need to let each utility company know that you have moved in so they can bill you accurately. If you decide that a phone is an essential part of life then you will also need to make arrangements to have that connected and the bills put in your name. Details of your nearest utilities offices will be in the local phone book. You should do all of this as soon as possible or you may find yourself being hassled for other people's debts because, unless you change the names on the account, the utilities companies will pursue the debts with the people living in the property regardless of who ran up the bill.

In shared houses you can ask the company to put all the residents' names on the bills, or divide the responsibility between you so that one person is named on the gas bill and another on the electricity. How you divide payment is up to your household to determine. You may find that you need to be flexible about this: it is difficult to tell when you first move in who is going to spend hours on the phone and who is going to use up all the hot water every morning by soaking in a luxurious bath.

It is easier to monitor phone calls if you live in an area where you can get itemised bills. These give the number called and the cost of the call for conversations costing more than 50p. You should also keep a book by the phone where everyone writes down how long they were on the phone for, what time of day it was and whether or not it was a local call. You can then work out who owes what by getting a book of rates from your local BT shop. It is more difficult to monitor individual use of other utilities so it is usually easier just to split the bills between the number of people living in the house. However, if there is one person who consistently uses more electricity or gas than the others you can also get a book of rates from the relevant utility company.

### The Council Tax

The Council Tax has now replaced the Community Charge or Poll Tax. Under the new legislation, students do not have to pay any Council Tax providing they live exclusively with other students. If there is one person in the house who is not a student then unfortunately the students in that house are jointly liable for the Council Tax with the person who is not a student. This is something you might want to consider when choosing who to share with.

You should make sure you obtain a Council Tax form from your council office, as the assumption will be that you are liable unless you inform them otherwise. The sooner you are registered as a student the less likely it is that you will be hounded by bills and court demands.

### Questions to ask when renting privately

❏ Will it be a joint tenancy agreement and how long will it be for?

❏ Will the landlord or the tenants choose co-tenants?

❏   How will I have to pay the rent?

❏   Will I need to pay rent in the vacations?

❏   How much is the deposit and can I have a signed receipt?

❏   Are bills included in the rent and will they be in my name?

❏   Will I have to arrange to have the utilities connected?

❏   How is the property heated and how much does it cost?

❏   What condition is the plumbing and wiring in?

❏   Have there been any major structural repairs in the last 12 months?

❏   What security provisions are there?

❏   What is the surrounding area like? (How far away are the shops/transport/supermarket, etc?)

❏   How frequently and how late does public transport run?

❏   When can I move in?

## Lodgings

6

I live with my Lithuanian landlord, which is very convenient and close to university. I have my own entrance and independence so I have stayed here for three years. The only slight drawback I have ever encountered was when I woke up one morning to find the BBC camped outside the front door. Apparently the local newspapers had run a story about my landlord being involved in Nazi war crimes.

9

*Fourth-year student, Edinburgh University*

The broad definition of a lodger is someone who lives with their landlord or landlady. You may live with a family, with someone who is struggling to pay the mortgage, or someone who rents to you cheaply in return for your baby-sitting services. Living with a family used to be a very common form of student accommodation but most students today find it too restrictive. However, if you are unsure about moving away from your parental home then this can be a good way to cushion the break.

If you do decide to live as a lodger then try to make sure you will get on well with the landlord or landlady and find out exactly what the house rules are and what you are paying for. Depending on the lodging arrangement, your rent may be more expensive than in other forms of private sector renting but it could include bills and food. It is particularly important that you get all details sorted out right at the start, as you will have to sign a licence agreement (see page 68).

## Council housing, housing associations and co-ops

These types of housing are much cheaper to rent but you are unlikely to fulfil the necessary requirements and will have to put your name on a long waiting list.

Council accommodation is unlikely to be given to single students and anyway some councils will want you to have lived in the borough for at least three years. However, it might be an option worth considering, particularly if you are a mature student with dependants or are a student with special needs. Your local town hall will be able to give you details and information and your students' union should know if there are any local schemes whose requirements you would fulfil.

Housing associations aim to provide cheap housing for specific groups of people and some do include single people in their categories. Again, you are more likely to find accommodation in this sector if you have special needs or are a mature student. Most housing associations also have long waiting lists, but your students' union or college accommodation office will be able to tell you if there are any worth putting your name down for.

Co-ops are run by groups of people who manage the property themselves. They are very difficult to join unless you know someone who is already living in a co-op: most places are filled by word of mouth.

## Emergency housing

There may be times when you find yourself without anywhere to live, or you may want to arrange short-term accommodation over the holiday period. If you are in this position then get a list of bed and breakfasts and hostels in the area from your accommodation office, students' union or the local phone book.

Hostels can be particularly useful if you find yourself without a roof over your head; some offer short-term lodging of up to 28 days, which should give you plenty of time to sort out some permanent housing. You should always ring before turning up expecting to be given a room because different hostels have different requirements. You do not really want to trek across town only to find that the hostel you have selected is single sex and you've got the wrong set of chromosomes!

There was a great deal of difference between the hostels I lived in. In the first one, where I shared a room with a friend of mine from the art college for about a term, we were allowed to cook food in the room and pretty much come and go as we pleased. The second hostel we lived in for about two weeks had much more rigorous rules. We were not allowed to cook our own food and had curfews.

*Second-year student, Edinburgh University*

Bed and breakfasts will not ask you to fulfil special criteria but will place limits on how long you can stay. They can also be very expensive, particularly if you have to eat out. Both bed and breakfasts and hostels should only ever be used as emergency accommodation. You should not try to live by moving from one place to another as this will seriously disrupt your study.

A small minority of students, mainly in London, have turned to squatting because they have found it impossible to afford the private sector rents. It is, at present, not illegal except in Scotland; however, if legislation goes through it soon will be. Breaking and entering is against the law wherever you are but provided squatters are not caught entering the property, and change the locks once they are in, they can stay there until they are evicted by the bailiffs. Before this happens, they are served with a summons to appear at a court hearing where the judge will grant the owner with a Court Order of Possession. Once this has been granted, the bailiffs are given a warrant which they will then use to evict the squatters.

We got about nine-tenths of the way into this house and then realised we were trying to squat a property directly opposite the local police station, which didn't seem like a screamingly sensible idea.

*Third-year student, University of London*

The quality of housing used by squatters is often very poor and there is very little security unless you can make sure there is someone in the house all the time. Squatting should definitely *not* be relied on as a housing option. Remember, you have no security against eviction and could find yourself homeless with very little notice.

## Making the right choice

You can use this table, in conjunction with the information contained in the chapter, as a guide to where you might be happiest living. Think carefully about the sort of person you are and be honest with yourself.

| Type of accommodation | Confident about leaving home | Independent | Wants to meet students | Wants to mix with non-students | Finds it difficult to mix | Unsure about leaving home |
|---|---|---|---|---|---|---|
| Halls (catered) | ★ | ★ | ★ | | ★ | ★ |
| Halls (self-catered) | ★ | ★ | ★ | | ★ | |
| Student houses/flats | ★ | ★ | ★ | | | |
| Student villages | ★ | ★ | ★ | | | |
| Private accommodation in student area | ★ | ★ | ★ | | | |
| Private accommodation in non-student area | ★ | ★ | | ★ | | |
| Lodger with family | | | | | ★ | ★ |
| Lodger not as part of a family | ★ | ★ | | ★ | | |
| Bedsit | ★ | ★ | | ★ | | |

Just because you don't allocate yourself many stars doesn't mean that you are going to find it more difficult to settle into university life, it just means you will have to give more thought to, and ask more questions about, your chosen form of accommodation.

# Lifesavers⊗

## Organisations

Your students' union and local independent housing advice centres are the best places to go to with contract or landlord problems. Look in the local phone book for details.

SHAC, 189a Old Brompton Road, London SW5 0AR, tel 071-373 7276. Gives advice and information on housing problems in the Greater London area. Also produces housing aid information leaflets.

Shelter Emergency Advice Line: tel 0800 446441. 88 Old Street, London EC1V 9HU, tel 071-253 0202. Gives advice to those needing housing and will put you in contact with local housing organisations.

Shelter (Cymru) Wales, 25 Walter Road, Swansea SA1 5NN, tel 0792 469400.

Shelter Northern Ireland, 165 University Street, Belfast BT7 1HR, tel 0232 247752.

Shelter Scotland, 65 Cockburn Street, Edinburgh EH1 1BU, tel 031-226 6347.

## Publications

*Law and Order in Private Rented Housing,* published by Campaign for Bedsit Rights, 7 Whitechapel Road, London E1 1DU, tel 071-377 0027. Free to tenants.

# 3 Living on Your Own – the Basics

Learning to live away from home and how to get to grips with things domestic can take some time. You may make some mistakes along the way but you are also likely to have a lot of fun as you discover a new sense of freedom. This chapter will provide a few pointers on how to avoid the most common pitfalls.

## What to take with you

What you take to university will largely depend on where you are going to be living. For example, if you live in a hall of residence you need far fewer domestic items than if you are renting a bedsit. Wherever you live, some posters and plants will personalise the place, but bear in mind the size of the room and remember you may have to travel by public transport. If you are living in rented or self-catered accommodation then compare what is already provided with what is suggested in the checklists.

I packed really late and took loads of knives and forks with me. I just dumped everything in the middle of the sitting room and crammed it into dustbin liners at the last minute. My grandparents came to see me last weekend and I had to give them five bin bags full of stuff I don't need.

*First-year student, Swansea University*

**General essentials (wherever you live)**
You must make sure you take with you:

❏ all correspondence you have ever received from the university, including course and reading lists, accommodation information and the letter of acceptance

❏ all correspondence you have from your grant allocation authority

❏ your National Insurance number and any tax forms you have

❏ your passport and birth certificate

❏ any medical certificates you have been asked to bring and/or your doctor's details

❏ your bank details

❏ an address book and phone cards

❏ a kettle and some mugs with a jar of coffee and a carton of longlife milk to get you started

❏ a corkscrew and bottle opener

❏ a tin opener

❏ a torch

❏ an alarm clock

❏ a soft toilet roll

❏ any medicines you need and some painkillers to cope with any initial hangovers

❏ toiletries

❏ lots of file paper and some files

❏ a dictionary and any general reference books you find useful

❏ pens, scissors, paper clips, a hole punch, Tipp-Ex, rubber, etc

❏ clothes, shoes and underwear. Don't be fooled by the fact that it might be a hot day when you pack. Make sure you leave room for a selection of jumpers. It's really miserable trying to write an essay while wrapped up in every available blanket. You will find that there are very few occasions when you will have to dress up. The student dress code is whatever you define it as. You will be able to spend your entire time at university in jeans and shapeless jumpers if you choose to, though a smart outfit for job interviews might be useful. You will, however, need to take lots of outdoor clothing with you as you will be spending more time waiting at bus stops and train stations: you can't ring for a parental taxi any more!

- ❏ towels (large and small)
- ❏ coat hangers
- ❏ bedding; this may be provided for you but you may prefer to take your own and take extra blankets.

## Optional extras (wherever you live)
Optional extras include:

- ❏ something to play music on. (Consider carefully whether you want to risk taking your expensive, precious music system and your prized CD collection with you. It's a better idea to take a portable cassette player and a selection of tapes.)
- ❏ plants
- ❏ posters and Blu-Tack
- ❏ one or two photos
- ❏ ornaments
- ❏ games (Trivial Pursuit, etc)
- ❏ a TV (for which you will need a licence)
- ❏ sports equipment

- [ ] reading lamps (note that some halls don't provide them)

- [ ] a personal computer: some courses may require work to be produced on one, although the university will probably provide access to a machine.

### Extras needed for catered halls of residence

You will need to take these basic cooking utensils with you as there will be occasions when you miss meal times or don't feel like eating hall meals:

- [ ] two plates
- [ ] bowls
- [ ] knives, forks and spoons
- [ ] a medium-sized saucepan
- [ ] a wooden spoon
- [ ] a sharp knife
- [ ] a toaster for independence from the kitchen and to save you having to get up in time for breakfast.

### Additional extras needed for self-catered halls or rented accommodation

Additional extras necessary include:

- [ ] a large saucepan
- [ ] a frying pan
- [ ] a colander
- [ ] a spatula
- [ ] a cheese grater
- [ ] a measuring jug
- [ ] more cutlery
- [ ] more crockery

❑   an oven-proof dish

❑   recipe books might also be useful

❑   more bedding, including lots of blankets or a duvet

❑   cleaning stuff for kitchens, bathrooms, floors, etc.

❑   some basic DIY tools such as a hammer, screw-drivers (small and large), an adjustable spanner, pliers, nails and screws

❑   light bulbs

❑   a heater

❑   fuse-wire (if the house has an old-fashioned fuse-box).

The key to planning what you should take is to consider carefully where you will be living. You don't want to end up hardly able to open your door because you have tried to move the contents of your parents' house into your room. On the other hand, you don't want to have to return home after a couple of days because you have forgotten to pack a spare pair of shoes.

Don't try to do all your packing on the night before you leave when you return from the pub after saying good-bye to your friends. Start at least two days before you go as this will give plenty of time think about what you are going to take.

# Setting up home

Assuming you have made the journey from home to university with all your belongings intact, there are going to be various domestic things you will need to sort out, particularly if your new home is rented in the private sector. You may want to put some tasks on a house rota.

## Getting the utilities connected

You should get the utility companies to read the meters on the day that you move in. If you don't you could find yourself landed with someone else's debts (see chapter 2, page 77).

All utility companies will offer you different methods of payment but tend to encourage direct debit, where the money is taken out of your bank account (usually in monthly instalments). This can cause some problems in a shared flat. You could set up an account in the name and address of your house into which everyone contributes. You should think about whether a standing order is the best way to pay as, by being careful, it is possible to save money on bills. If you decide to pay by standing order you should make sure your meters are read regularly to check your usage is being charged accurately. You should discuss how you are going to pay for utilities before you all move in.

Do not panic if you get an unexpectedly high bill. Companies do make mistakes and they can often be sorted out over the phone. If you are not satisfied with the treatment you receive then contact the complaints organisations listed at the end of each section.

### Electricity

There is no connection charge for electricity unless there are any outstanding debts. If this is the case then you should talk to your landlord and get him to sort it out. If the bills are going to be in your name then you should contact the local electricity board (it will be listed in the phone book) and tell them you have moved in. You should do this on the first day your contract runs from. If you are a first-time customer, you will either be asked for a deposit or to pay by standing order. A deposit shared between flatmates is probably a better idea than leaving one person with the responsibility of finding the money.

We got a £680 electricity bill once because they read the meter wrongly. When my flatmate phoned them to query this they tried to persuade her that the bill was not unreasonable, even though our cooker and heating were gas. They eventually agreed to send someone else round to read the meter and they managed to read it wrongly again. When I got back I took the correct meter reading and it was all sorted out relatively quickly. I couldn't believe two electricity board people managed to read an electricity meter wrong twice.

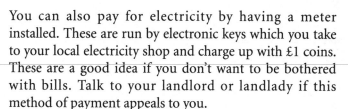

*Fouth-year student, Edinburgh University*

You can also pay for electricity by having a meter installed. These are run by electronic keys which you take to your local electricity shop and charge up with £1 coins. These are a good idea if you don't want to be bothered with bills. Talk to your landlord or landlady if this method of payment appeals to you.

If you don't pay your bills then the electricity will be cut off and you will then be liable for an extra charge for reconnecting the supply. Once you are identified as a bad payer you are likely to be offered a prepayment meter as an alternative way of payment if you don't already have one.

If you have any complaints then contact OFFER, whose address is in the Lifesavers section at the end of this chapter.

## Gas

The gas supply should already be connected when you move in. If it isn't, ring the local board and find out if there are any outstanding bills for your address. If there are then you need to contact your landlord or landlady immediately and get him or her to sort it out. You can also be cut off for non-payment of gas bills and you will be charged a reconnection fee.

Faulty gas appliances can be very dangerous (see chapter 2, page 64). If you smell gas then put out any cigarettes or candles, do not turn on any lights because the switches can cause sparks, get out of the property and contact the local gas board IMMEDIATELY.

If you have any complaints then contact OFGAS, which is the watchdog for all the gas companies.

## Water

If you get a bill for the water rates it is likely to be addressed to 'the Occupier'. This is not likely to mean you, although you should check your contract. Pass it on to your landlord or landlady.

OFWAT are the people to contact with any complaints.

## Telephone

You shouldn't have any problems getting a phone connected as most households already have a telephone line, but you will have to pay a standard charge per quarter (currently £23.68 for a line and £4.99 to rent a telephone). To have a telephone line installed you will have to pay £116.32. If you haven't been a BT customer before you may also have to pay a deposit. Deposits vary according to the area and your standing as a BT customer and are up to the discretion of the local BT office.

You can do certain things to reduce the cost of having a phone installed. BT will rent you a pay phone or, if you live in an area where the digital exchange system operates, you can arrange to have a phone which will only accept incoming calls. If you regularly make long distance or overseas calls then it is worth getting a phone with a Mercury button. These reduce the cost of your calls by some 40 per cent and you can get fully itemised bills for Mercury calls. Look out for the advertisements or in the local phone book for details of your nearest office.

If you do decide to have a phone installed then get hold of a copy of the free leaflet *Your Guide to Telephone Charges* which explains the different rates and is available from your local BT district office (listed in the phone book). As a general rule of thumb, avoid making calls before 6 pm. Evenings and weekends are the cheap rate periods. You should ask if your bill can be itemised and keep a book by the phone where everyone writes down where and when they called and how long they were on the phone for. This will save arguments when you come to divide up your first three-figure phone bill.

If you do not pay your account then you will be cut off seven days after the date on the last red bill. This bill will also have an 'expiry date', after which the charges for reconnection increase. If you are cut off on a regular basis or leave it too long after the expiry date, then you may be asked to pay a deposit before BT will reconnect you.

Contact OFTEL with any complaints you have.

## TV and video rentals

Many companies offer students special offers, especially at the beginning of the academic year. You should shop around to get the best deal, but stick to well-known companies. You may be asked for a deposit or to pay by standing order and your name will definitely be given to the TV licensing authority. To get a TV licence, go to the Post Office and pick up the relevant form. If you are going to rent a television and/or a video then you should do this at the beginning of the year as short-term rentals are more expensive.

## Laundry

Sooner or later you are going to have to get around to washing your clothes. The cheapest place to do this will be in your students' union or hall of residence laun-derette. There will be some very simple instructions for you to follow so the only thing you will need to worry about is whether you can trust people not to walk off with your jeans while you go to your lecture.

You will need to separate your clothes into whites, coloureds and delicates (woollens and synthetics). You can wash both whites and coloureds on a warm or medium wash but delicates need a cool wash. You might prefer not to trust precious items to the machine and wash them by hand, which is also a cheaper option. If you do decide to do this then you shouldn't wring them out as it pulls them out of shape. In fact, it's a good idea not to trust anything delicate to launderettes as they are always too hot: perfect for jeans and T-shirts, though. If you have any doubts look at the washing instructions on the label and match them to the machine's programmes.

Different people have different attitudes to ironing. Some people have a positive aversion to ironing and others are quite fanatical about ironing everything down to their socks and sheets. If you are an ironing person then successfully completing a wash means you have to acquire a talent for ironing. You will avoid all ironing disasters by making sure you follow the codes on the labels. Find the picture of the iron and see how many dots it has on it. One dot means you need a cool iron, two a medium and three a hot one.

# DIY for beginners

There are bound to be things which go wrong during the time you rent a property. Anything major is likely to be the responsibility of the landlord or landlady and you should contact them immediately if the bathroom floods or the tiles start flying off the roof. It is, however, useful to have a basic knowledge of DIY to save time and keep you in your landlord's good books. You can buy beginners' guides from bookshops and DIY stores.

After living in the house for two months we started to notice cockroaches. We put down powder around the doors and windows and didn't notice anything for two months but, after that, there were swarms of them. We contacted the council which told us that they were Oriental cockroaches and carry the most diseases. We put down the powder they gave us, but it was too late. Before we realised it we had the biggest cockroach infestation in Brighton and had to move out of the house so it, and the furniture, could be fumigated.

*Second-year student, University of Brighton*

### Wiring a plug

Most people will have their own memory joggers to help them remember what goes where. A very simple one is to realise that the BLUE wire goes into the Bottom Left connection, the BROWN wire goes into the Bottom Right connection and the yellow and green one into what is left, the top centre connection. When you connect the wires, tightly fasten the screws on to the exposed section of wire so that when you pull the wires they do not move. Make sure that the gripper at the base of the plug is fastened across the outer cable and not the three wires.

Make sure you read the label attached to the appliance carefully and that your plug matches the fuse requirement. Most large household appliances need 13 amp fuses, and so do things like kettles, fan heaters, toasters and vacuum cleaners. Appliances like hairdryers, hi-fi systems and desk lamps operate at much lower wattage and take 3 amp fuses.

## Changing a fuse

If you have changed the plug and the appliance still isn't working or the lights in one part of the house refuse to come on, then you have probably got a blown fuse. Go to the main fuse box and check what amp fuse is needed. You MUST turn off the mains switch before you touch any fuses. You will know if you have got the right switch because the whole house will be plunged into darkness. Old houses have fuse-wires which are more tricky to change than contact breakers but the principle is the same: remove the broken wire and replace it with fuse-wire of the correct thickness. Keep a torch by the fuse box so you can see what you are doing. If changing a fuse doesn't work then it will be a job for an electrician.

## Blocked sinks and frozen pipes

A sink plunger is a useful gadget to have. Sinks can get blocked quite frequently, especially when several people are all trying to force the remains of their supper down them. A plunger will often release the trapped waste. Place it over the plug hole and pump quickly about ten times. Pull the plunger up again and see if the sink empties. Repeat several times and then give up. Pipes can object quite violently to having fat or fatty waste poured down them, so don't do it: unblocking a sink or a pipe is not a pleasant task.

If the plunger fails, the pipe could be frozen or may have supper remains trapped in the overflow outlet. You could try heating the overflow outlet with a hairdryer if it's frozen or taking it off and removing what you find. If this still doesn't work then get help. Make sure you put a bucket under the U-bend before removing anything or you will be standing ankle-deep in water before you know it.

Your landlord should really deal with the insulation but you can also take preventive measures to stop pipes freezing if there is a cold spell coming on by wrapping the pipes in old rags and fastening them with string. Freezing pipes can be quite a problem in some parts of the country.

It is a good idea to know where the stopcock, which turns the water mains off, is in case of an emergency. There may be more than one and they may affect different rooms. Practise shutting the water off before you have a major flood.

### Changing a washer

If you have a leaking tap or one which shoots water at you violently every time you turn it on, then you will need a new washer. Turn off the water at the stopcock and unscrew the tap. You will find a rubber circle between the tap and the mounting. Take the washer to your local hardware store or DIY shop and find one which matches it. Put the tap back together again with the new washer.

## Food

Food is something which all too often gets forgotten in the student lifestyle. However, this is not a good idea as you can't fully participate in things if you lack energy because your diet is poor.

There are numerous theories about what exactly constitutes a good diet and opinions seem to change every six months. You will not be able to follow the latest fads on a

LIBRARY
BISHOP BURTON COLLEGE
BEVERLEY HU17 8QG

student grant. You should stick to the general principle that your diet needs to consist of:

●▸ carbohydrates – bread, pasta, rice, potatoes

●▸ protein – meat, fish, eggs, pulses

●▸ fat

●▸ vitamins

●▸ fibre.

Eat 'peasant-style' and base your meal around carbohydrates and vegetables. Added protein can be supplied by a little meat, poultry or fish or, if you're vegetarian, eggs, cheese, dried beans and lentils. Fresh fruit will provide extra vitamins and fibre.

You should make sure you eat at least two good meals a day, preferably three. Fill yourself up on bread and potatoes rather than chocolate and biscuits. Carbohydrates provide better nutrition, are cheaper and are less fattening. Never ever cut back on food as a way of saving money. It will make you ill and, if your health suffers, your social and academic life will suffer too. For ways to eat cheaply, see the Budgeting section in chapter 1.

I had some very strange eating habits in my first year. My staple diet was spaghetti. Very sophisticated you might think – not the way I cooked it. Spaghetti a la margarino con poco des tutti les spices I could find in the Italian shop near college. I fried the spaghetti and ate it in the early hours of the morning, just before I went to bed, at least four times a week for three terms. Very nice? Revolting.

*Third-year student, University of London*

You can usually spot who has gone to university by the food they cook. Some 'stock' student recipes are given below. They can combine any variety of ingredients and all cost under £1 per helping. The most important thing to remember if you are learning to cook for yourself is not to be afraid to experiment. The wonderful thing about student recipes is that, even if you are the most inept person ever to set foot in a kitchen, you cannot go wrong.

## Essential cupboard items

These are the items you should keep in your kitchen. They are also the things you should ask your parents to buy if they offer to send you off to college with a food parcel. A stock of chocolate biscuits may be comforting but it won't last long and isn't very nutritious.

| | |
|---|---|
| Pasta | Salt and pepper |
| Rice | Stock cubes |
| Lentils | Margarine/butter |
| Tins of tomatoes | Milk |
| Tomato purée | Bread |
| Kidney beans | Jam/marmalade |
| Baked beans | A tin of fish (tuna, sardines). |
| Onions | Buy fish in oil as you can cook |
| Oil | with the oil, which not only |
| Flour | saves money, but adds flavour |
| Mixed herbs | to food. |
| Garlic | |

## Recipes

### Pasta sauce

Mastering this sauce is really easy. You can pour it over pasta on its own or with any combination of vegetables, meat or fish.

Take a tablespoon of margarine or butter and gently melt it in a large pan. Take the pan off the heat. Very gradually, add enough flour to absorb all the margarine. Stir all the time so that there are no lumps. Return it to a low heat and cook for about two minutes. Take off the heat again and gradually add a pint of milk, stirring vigorously all the time so you don't get any lumps. At this point you can add cheese, herbs, garlic, tuna fish, mustard, nutmeg or anything else you fancy. Return to the heat to gently heat through. (This is enough for at least two people – even for four if you mix it with lots of pasta.)

An even simpler pasta sauce can be made by frying your chosen vegetables until soft, then adding a tin of tomatoes, with herbs and seasoning to taste.

### Pasta bake

This is alternatively known as pasta 'à la whatever happens to be in the fridge', as, providing the ingredients are edible, you can literally add whatever you want!

Cook the pasta by following the instructions on the packet and adding two teaspoons of oil (this will stop the pasta sticking together). Fry the vegetables, tuna fish, bacon or whatever you like with salt, pepper and any other herbs or seasonings. Mix with the pasta. Put the pasta and vegetables, etc, into an oven-proof dish, pour a pint of the sauce over it and put into a medium oven (gas mark 4/350°F/180°C) for about 15 minutes until the top goes crispy. Alternatively you can just pour a cheese sauce over plain pasta or stir a tin of soup into your fried ingredients and serve over the pasta immediately. Particularly good ingredients for this recipe are sweetcorn, tomatoes, onions, carrots, tuna and, if you feel like treating yourself, mushrooms and peppers. This dish stores well so you can make a lot and eat it again the next day.

### Risotto

Again, this is a recipe to which you can add any variety of ingredients. A good rule of thumb when cooking rice is that you need 1½ times as much water to rice. Half a cup of rice will feed one person.

Fry your chosen vegetables, meat or fish in a large pan. When they are nearly cooked, add the rice and a table-spoon of tomato purée and fry for about two minutes. Dissolve a stock cube in the water (you will need more than one if you are cooking for more than one person) and add the stock to the pan. Add salt and pepper to taste. You can add kidney beans at this stage (dried beans are cheaper than tinned but need to be soaked first and simmered for an hour and a half before being added to the other ingredi-ents). Bring to the boil, turn down the heat, then cover the pan and leave it to simmer for the length of time your rice packet says the rice needs to be cooked, checking it every now and again to check it's not boiling over or sticking. If there is any excess water left after the rice is cooked, take the lid off and boil the water away.

## Soup

Soups are very nutritious, very easy to make and will feed you for three days. Choose whatever you fancy to make your soup. Seasonal root vegetables are particularly good and make very cheap soups.

Fry, steam or boil your ingredients. Add enough water to cover your ingredients. Add a couple of stock cubes, salt, pepper and any herbs. Leave to simmer until it reduces in quantity and the solid ingredients soften. Put through a blender or mouli if you have one and like smooth soup. Serve with a chunk of fresh bread.

For a special occasion you can add cream to the soup and make some garlic butter for your bread (just crush a few cloves of garlic and mix them with butter; cut slices into a French stick, leaving them joined at the bottom, and spread both sides with the garlic butter; bake in a hot oven for ten minutes).

## Jacket potatoes

Jacket potatoes are the easiest meal to cook. All you have to do is wash the potatoes and prick their skins with a fork a couple of times. Put them in a hot oven (gas mark 7/425°F/270°C), check them after 45 minutes and every 10 minutes after that. You will know when they are cooked when the skins go crispy and you can easily put a fork or a skewer through the potato.

Add anything from cheese and baked beans to tuna and mayonnaise. You can make jacket potatoes special by scooping out the potato from the skins, mixing it with your ingredients, putting it back into the skins and heating the potatoes under a hot grill for a few minutes. Serve jacket potatoes with omelettes, meat, burgers or on their own.

## Pancakes

Pancakes are not just for Shrove Tuesday, to be sprinkled with lemon and sugar. They are extremely cheap and versatile. You can put any variety of fried savoury ingredients into a pancake as well as the more traditional sweet fillings.

Sieve together four heaped tablespoons of flour with ¼ teaspoon of salt or sugar depending on whether you prefer your pancake savoury or sweet. Add two standard-sized eggs and mix into the flour. Gradually stir in ¼ pint of milk and beat thoroughly until well mixed. Add the rest of the milk and beat again. It's a good idea to leave batter for at least ten minutes before you use it. Heat just enough oil to barely cover the surface of the frying pan. Pour in enough batter to just cover the surface. Cook for about two minutes on each side until light brown.

## Health warning

NEVER eat anything past the use-by date.

NEVER leave food out, particularly if it is cooked.

NEVER eat anything with mould on it. It is not good enough just to cut the mouldy bits off as mould puts down long roots. Throw it away.

ALWAYS store raw meat at the bottom of the fridge below cooked food.

ALWAYS reheat food to 70°C (very hot) in the centre for at least two minutes.

ALWAYS wash the work surface in between preparing different foodstuffs, particularly if you are preparing meat.

ALWAYS keep the kitchen clean.

ALWAYS contact the local council's pest control department immediately if you spot any pests.

# Lifesavers ☣

## Organisations

You will need to get the numbers and addresses of your local council departments from the phone book. Look under the name of your council and the relevant departments and trading standards authorities will be listed.

Consumers' Association, 2 Marylebone Road, London NW1 4DX, tel 071-486 5544.

National Association of Citizens' Advice Bureaux (NACAB), Myddleton House, 115–123 Pentonville Road, London N1 9LZ, tel 071-833 2181. You should look in the phone book for the number and address of your local branch which can give independent advice and information on all problems, from personal to debt.

National Debt Line, tel 021-359 8501.

Office of Electricity Regulation (OFFER), Hagley House, 83–85 Hagley Road, Edgbaston, Birmingham B16 0QG, tel 021-456 2100.

Office of Gas Supply (OFGAS), Stockley House, 130 Wilton Road, London SW1V 9LQ, tel 071-828 0898.

Office of Telecommunications (OFTEL), 50 Ludgate Hill, London EC4M 7JJ, tel 071-822 1650.

Office of Water Services (OFWAT), Centre City Tower, 7 Hill Street, Birmingham B5 4UA, tel 021-625 5608.

## Publications

*Grub on a Grant*, Headline, £4.99
*The Student Cookbook*, Collins and Brown, £4.99
*The Bean Book*, Fontana/Collins, £5.99

# 4 Your First Term

## Freshers' week

Freshers' week is something that should only happen to sane people once in their lifetime. You will be hurled into a whirlwind of social and organisational activity and will emerge wondering when it was that you last had a decent night's sleep or a meal. Don't worry if this sounds daunting: everybody is in exactly the same boat and most people thoroughly enjoy themselves.

You will be sent detailed instructions for when you first arrive so make sure you bring this information with you. Don't worry about not being able to find your way around, as there will be plenty of signs and people to direct you.

You will be told where you need to go to register (sign on as a student). The first point of contact varies in different institutions. Some will want you to register with your students' union, some with the accommodation office, if you have been allocated a place in college accommodation, and some with the university.

By the end of your first few days you should have registered with your students' union, your faculty and department, the health centre or a doctor and the library, and made sure you have picked up your grant cheque and found out about applying for a student loan and access fund (see chapter 1). You will acquire several cards along the way, including a college card – which will usually also serve as your library card – and a card showing you are a member of your students' union. Bring at least four passport-sized photographs with you as each card you are issued will require one.

You should make sure you have readily accessible any communication you have ever received from the university and the authority responsible for allocating your grant as you will need to be able to produce these as proof that you should be there and are entitled to your grant. Make sure you have taken photocopies of all communications and keep them safe, just in case anything goes wrong and you need additional proof.

You may be given a formal welcome by the university where members of staff introduce themselves and give you a few useful tips on what to do and what to avoid. But, basically, you will spend your first days trying to get your bearings, settling into your accommodation and meeting the other new students.

Don't worry if you don't get on immediately with the people you are living with. University accommodation offices have differing policies on allocating rooms. Just because you have meticulously filled in an accommodation questionnaire doesn't necessarily mean that you have been placed with your perfect partners; but remember, it does take time to settle in.

You will probably spend your first few days doing what seems to be an endless coffee round, crammed into small student study rooms, if you're lucky sitting on the one chair provided for guests, but more likely sitting on the floor, while you establish who you like and who you don't.

### Freshers' activities run by students' unions

Your students' union will have organised at least one event – probably in the evening of your first day – to help you meet the other students.

We organise our freshers' week so that no new student has time to think. By the time they emerge at the other end they know lots of people without having to make an effort or realising that is what is happening. We

also make sure they have a great time and
there is always a choice for people.

*Welfare Officer, Bangor University*

You will probably be offered the chance of buying a card
which will allow you in to all the students' union organised activities during the freshers' period. These can be
good value for money if you like the sound of the events
offered and you are pretty sure you are not going to lose
your card during the revelry. They sometimes also provide discounts at local cinemas, shops and other outlets
(you may also get these discounts with your union card).

I stood in the union thinking "what have I
done?" But the great thing about being flung
into this situation is that you aren't really left
with any other option than to take a deep
breath and get on with it. Which is precisely
what I did and had one of the best times
ever. I don't think I'd ever had to choose
between three things to do in one evening
before.

*Third-year student, University of London*

The nature of these events will depend entirely upon the
imagination and energy of the people running your students' union and can range from organised quiz and
game shows to spontaneous pub crawls. Try to avoid
events which are not organised by the union as they may
be a rip-off.

You should definitely join in at least one of the events
organised, even if you are unsure about meeting new
people. The later you leave it, the harder it will be to make
friends because people will have begun to form groups.
Remember that initially everybody is in the same position

and will be as nervous as each other, even if some are better at hiding it. You will probably surprise yourself and end up having a really good time.

My next-door neighbour, I decided, was going to be tall, dark, mysterious and probably called Jean-Paul. What I actually got was a girl with a Fireman Sam duvet cover, which I could have forgiven if it were not for the Sam posters on the wall and her desire to be a fire-fighter when she "grew up". It just goes to show that universal toleration is one of the most important things university teaches you.

*Second-year student, Durham University*

Most students' unions will organise a freshers' ball. These are not usually formal affairs but are just an excuse (not that you will tend to need one) for an all-night party with a mixture of live music, discos and extended bar licences. It may be held towards the end of the freshers' introduction period and be open to students from other years. This is a very good way of getting to meet other students at the university.

### Freshers' fairs

These are also known as Intro Fairs, or even 'Fayres' in those universities with olde worlde pretensions. They are the places where you can find out all about the clubs and societies your university has to offer and where you will be bombarded by companies with 'student interests' plying you with freebies to attract your custom. The companies who take stalls at freshers' fairs can range from the Armed Forces to the local cinema, from banks to magazines. The first thing to do is find the company that is giving away the largest plastic bag; you will need it to put all the freebies in.

I went round my freshers' fair in a state of complete confusion and amazement. I ended up joining a martial arts club which I couldn't even pronounce and the English club out of a sense of duty. I didn't go to any meetings of either but stuck to just two of the ten clubs I had managed to join. I'd paid at least another three pints of beer in membership fees.

*First-year student, University of London*

Most universities offer an impressive range of sports and extracurricular activities and there is bound to be something which interests you. You can try anything from karate to cricket or meditation to step aerobics. If there isn't already a club catering for your hobby or interest, then you should think about setting one up (see page 115).

You should be wary of over-enthusiastic club members who are trying hard to persuade you to join their activity. You may have to pay a fee to join, so make sure you have looked at the list of stalls and have a rough idea of those you might be interested in before you launch yourself into joining anything. The students' union may well publish a handbook which will give you more specific details about the club's or society's past history, successes and meeting times. Clubs and societies are great places to meet people with whom you share a commmon interest, but if you are asked for money, make sure you know where the money goes and what you will be getting for it.

When I joined the drama society I found that, not only did I meet people who shared my interest in theatre, but I also got to meet their friends. Before long I knew an awful lot of people around the campus.

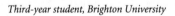

*Third-year student, Brighton University*

## Departmental events

You will be given a list of what your department has organised either when you register or through your pigeon hole, which is where you will collect all your post. Some departments are very keen on arranging social events and you will be bombarded with invitations to meet the head of department, your personal tutor and every single lecturer you might ever possibly encouter during your time at university.

I think I found my department cheese and wine party useful. I hadn't actually been to bed for three days so I doubt whether I was exactly sparkling. I don't really like formal, best-behaviour occasions but it was quite useful to be a recognised face. It meant my department didn't seem so alien.

*Second-year student, Oxford University*

Departmental get-togethers can be very useful: some people find it helpful to get to know their lecturers in a social context before they confront them in a classroom. Even if this idea does not appeal to you, departmental parties are good places to meet other students. It is useful to be able to identify one or two faces you know are on the same course, even if you just end up comparing timetable arrangements or lecture hall locations.

## Finding your way around

You will probably not be expected to attend any classes until at least three days after you arrive so that you have time to sort out where you should be and when you should be there. Departmental secretaries are extremely helpful people during this time and you should go to them with any queries and not be afraid to ask; they will undoubtedly have been asked the same thing before.

I have absolutely no sense of direction and was still blundering my way round college in the second term. This is not a good way to make an impression. I solved the problem by arranging to go to lectures with someone on my course who was living in the same hall of residence.

*Second-year student, University of London*

When you register with your faculty and department you will be told what introductory talks are being held, where you can find your timetable, how to select your options, and you will probably be given a map of the department's lecture rooms and classrooms. You won't be expected to know where you are going immediately. You should leave extra time to get to lectures until you find your bearings, but don't worry too much about being late because you got lost. You will receive a sympathetic reception during the first two weeks. However, you probably won't get quite such a warm reception if you are still getting lost halfway through the first term.

You may also be invited to go on a tour of the library. This might seem like an unnecessary thing to fit into a very busy schedule and it is not usually very enthralling, but it is useful, particularly in colleges which have large library facilities. You will probably be very glad to know where to go for the books relevant to your subject, how to use the cataloguing system and the various facilities available (see chapter 5), especially if your school or local library didn't have such good equipment. You should also take any opportunity to learn how to use the technology available (PCs, etc).

## Getting to know the area

Some universities run tours of the area where you will be shown the student haunts and the places to avoid. If you aren't offered such a tour then you should explore for yourself with your new friends. If you are living in a self-catering hall or house you will have to do this almost as soon as you get there. It is a good idea to ask students who are already at the university where the best local shops are and if there are any markets where you can buy food cheaply.

# Getting involved in university life

Many students miss the wealth of opportunities available in universities because their only involvement with college life is a regular spot at the bar, or a seat in the library. It is well worth exploring what your university can offer you apart from regular hangovers and a good degree.

Students' unions provide a wide range of sports clubs, societies and services for their students. Joining in some of the activities is an excellent way to make new friends who have similar interests to you. It can also provide you with some very valuable work experience. Employers are very impressed with people who have used all the opportunities available to them. You are also likely to have a lot of fun if you get involved with the students' union, a club or a society.

The great thing about going to university is that it is possible to do something completely new. Nobody knows you, so if there is something you have always fancied doing but have been afraid it would not fit in with your image, now is the time to take it up. As with all of university life, you get more out of your free time the more you put in.

## Sports clubs

> The football team went to Coventry to play a cup game. They went to the pitch where the game was to be played, saw a team and a referee, played the game and won 3–1. They returned home only to find that they had played Warwick University and qualified for the next round in the wrong league.

*Second-year student, Brighton University*

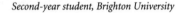

Sport is very big in many universities in terms of the numbers of students who get involved and the amount of money it attracts. The clubs that students' unions run vary around the country but there will always be several sports you can choose from.

The best time to join a sports club is at your freshers' fair. All clubs will have a stand there staffed by a member of the club whom you can talk to about meetings, training schedules and matches. If you miss joining the club of your choice at the freshers' fair, then you can contact it through the pigeon holes in the union. You will usually be able to join at any point during the year.

Most clubs will cater for all levels of experience, from complete beginners to those who are already well advanced. If you want to play sport seriously at university or continue an interest such as music or drama then contact the club as soon as possible as trials and auditions tend to be held in the first few weeks of term.

It is the most integrated club on campus. I joined the tennis club to improve my tennis for a dirt cheap membership fee. I have great quality coaching every week, challenging opposition, free travel, excellent aerobic and fitness circuit training as well as numerous social opportunities to get to know the national players. I learnt from these that the club provided much more than facilities for the simple beginner. The amount of coaching for élite players made me proud to be a member of Loughborough Tennis Club.

*Second-year student, Loughborough University*

If your students' union does not provide a club for the sport you want to play then you may be able to set one up. Go to the person responsible for administering sports clubs in your union and ask them what you need to do. The rules vary from place to place but you will usually have to collect a number of signatures from people also interested in such a club, outline how it would be run and present this to the committee which allocates budgets to sports clubs. Once you have your money you are up and running.

## Societies

Your students' union will also run societies for students who don't have sporting inclinations. These really can cover the whole spectrum and you can join anything from the *Magic Roundabout* club to the meditation society.

When you get to university you can use the societies on offer either to continue with an interest you already have or to try something completely new. They are an extremely good way to make friends in a relaxed and sociable atmosphere. Go along to your freshers' fair and have a look at the societies on offer.

"Chocolate is the root of all evil" is what the debating society last concluded. The speaker provided a particularly amusing argument for the motion in which he claimed that chocolate was not only bad for your health, but also had hallucinogenic effects. More importantly he insisted it was the cause of most international conflicts.

*Second-year student, Hull University*

The way you go about setting up a society will be similar to the way you go about setting up a sports club. It is worth taking time to plan properly as you are much more likely to be allowed to start up a society if you show you have put some thought into it, and if your predicted budgets balance. You should contact your students' union for specific details.

## Entertainments

This is probably the area most students get involved with. What is offered will depend entirely on where you are studying but 'Ents' (entertainments) are definitely a big part of all students' unions. Some unions have excellent reputations as gig venues and you will have the opportunity to see up-and-coming bands cheaply just before they make it big. Other unions will focus on getting local bands in and running regular discos. You will also be able to go and see plays, cabaret, listen to classical music and take part in quiz nights in your union.

If you want to have a say in the entertainments run by your union then you should find out whether there is an Ents committee. This is the committee which sets the agenda in conjunction with a sabbatical officer and/or a member of staff. This can be a very popular thing to get involved in so you should be quick if you are interested.

There can be certain perks to being an Ents officer, such as free gig passes, but you will probably also find yourself cleaning up the mess long after most people have gone to bed!

## Rag

Rag is extremely big in some unions. It incorporates all events students' unions run to raise money for charity. You may be approached at some point and asked to do anything from a three-legged pub crawl, to sitting on a bed while you are wheeled down the High Street. Medical students have a particularly strong reputation in the rag field and will go to extraordinary lengths to raise money.

Most universities will hold an annual Rag Week where the rag activities are concentrated into seven days of bizarre and wacky events all in the name of charity. You will usually be able to pick up a copy of a Rag Mag during this time and there may well be a Rag Ball. Other universities, like Loughborough and Aberystwyth, collect throughout the year, get most of their students involved and raise huge amounts of money.

### Student community action

This is growing in universities around the country. It offers students the chance to work with people in the local community. This can range from helping in homes for the elderly or mentally handicapped to helping run youth and school projects. It is a great way of getting to know your local community better and opening your mind to life outside the closed world of college. It will also impress future employers. Ask your union whether it has such a scheme.

### Student media

All universities have their own student newspaper or magazine. These may have a sabbatical editor or be run entirely by full-time students. They are an extremely good way for people with ambitions to be a journalist to get some practical experience, especially as some of them are held in high esteem by the national media. Any future employer will ask you to prove that you have already gained some experience in the media, as jobs in this field are so competitive. This applies to whatever area interests you, whether design, sub-editing, layout or writing. Your local paper may also be more willing to give you work experience opportunities if you have already worked on your student paper.

People who get involved with their student media will have the opportunity to attend the annual Student Media Conference which is hosted by the NUS in association with *The Guardian*. The conference provides opportunities to network, attend workshops, hone your skills and rub shoulders with big names in the media.

You may find you are able to get experience in other aspects of the media if your union runs a radio or television station. These are comparatively rare but you could try offering your services to the local hospital radio if you are interested in pursuing this career path.

## Students' unions

It can be very confusing when you first get to university to try and sort out exactly what role is played by the students' union. This is because its activities are so varied. It is easier to understand if you break them down into two main functions: services and representation. Services are all the things like bars, shops and sporting facilities which the students' union manages together with a wealth of sources of advice on accommodation, finance, welfare and so on. Representation basically includes anything which the students at the university have expressed a need for and can range from refining equal opportunities to discussing course problems with the university. In Scotland this divide is more marked in that there are two separate bodies which fulfil these functions: the union runs the services and the student association looks after the representation side, though both are run and managed by the same body of elected officers and employed managers working together.

I remember sitting in an academic council meeting surrounded by grey haired, grey suited (male) academics, and realising that the last time I had been in that room I had climbed over the roof and in through the window to protest about departmental cuts. This struck me as such a neat example of the two sides of student politics that I couldn't concentrate on the meeting at all!

*Third-year student, University of London*

To complicate matters further, different unions have different names for the same things. For instance, students' unions are also known as guilds of students and students' associations, and the meetings they hold to decide policy can be called anything from union general meetings, to the very odd-sounding general body meetings.

However, the basic structure is the same in all students' unions. There will be a number of sabbatical officers (which will differ according to the size of the university) who are responsible for the general running of the union. Sabbaticals are salaried officers who were all students when they were elected, so are very much in tune with the needs of students at their university. The job titles of sabbatical officers vary from one union to the next. Generally though, there will be sabbatical officers responsible for education matters, welfare, representation, sports, societies, entertainments and the finances of the union. Some student newspapers also have sabbatical editors. The way these areas of responsibility are divided among the sabbaticals will depend largely on how many sabbatical officers your union has, but their job titles are usually quite self-explanatory so you should be able to sort out who is responsible for what.

Sabbaticals are helped by an executive committee of students who are elected to help the sabbaticals with anything from approving budgets to setting policy, running the entertainments to making up posters. The members of the executive committee all have different job titles and areas of responsibility too. You will usually find that it is an executive member who has responsibility for women, overseas students, mature students and part-time students. There may also be executive officers who have no specific area of responsibility and are there to help out generally. The sabbaticals and executive are all accountable to the students at the university.

There are also staff members in each union who provide specialist services, advice and administrative support and help carry out the policies set by the students at the university via the various committees. The idea behind this structure is that students' unions are run as closely as possible to the wishes of the students they are there to serve.

Many students are put off getting involved with their students' union because the media still tend to portray politically motivated students as militant, angry young people who are determined to be as antagonistic as possible. In reality this is not the case. The political spectrum of students' unions reflects all shades of opinion and in recent years there has been a very strong move away from recognised political parties towards an independent stance. The idea behind this is that the needs of students should be put before any political agendas. However, if you enjoy political debate, you will have no trouble finding a forum, usually within various political societies within the union.

You can get involved with your students' union at many levels. You can go along to one of the union general meetings, where union policy is debated, or stand for election to a committee you have a particular interest in. You should not be put off if you have difficulty following the first meeting you attend. The regulations which govern these meetings can be confusing for even the most seasoned union officer, but it won't be long before you can sort through the jargon and understand the proceedings.

Most unions have a policy of allowing any student of the university to attend the general meetings, in fact they will positively welcome you with open arms. Any committee positions will be well advertised in the union buildings. You will need to get a nomination form signed and draw up a manifesto. You will then attend the electoral meeting and make a short speech outlining your ideas and beliefs. After that it is up to the meeting whether you are elected to that position or not.

You will find that getting involved with your student's union will give you many opportunities to exercise responsibility, leadership and organisational skills, and to make positive changes and contributions to your university on behalf of students, all of which will impress future employers. You will also end up having a lot of fun, particularly if you are someone who enjoys identifying problems and finding ways of solving them.

## The National Union of Students

As the law stands, you will automatically become a member of the National Union of Students if the university you attend is affiliated. If you study in Wales, Scotland or Northern Ireland then you become a member of the UCMC, NUS Scotland or NUS Northern Ireland respectively.

However, you need to watch national and student press for changes in this situation, as the government is thinking of introducing legislation which would alter it. Under the proposals students would automatically have access to a group of core services (like catering, welfare and representation), but would elect to use other non-core services (as yet undefined). The relationship of your students' union to the NUS under the proposals is not clear.

The NUS provides publications, advice, information, training and services for students' unions across the country, regional branches supplying this on a more localised basis. They are involved with representing students' views to national and government organisations.

The NUS holds one conference a year where national policies are set and elections held. Your NUS regional branch will also have an annual conference to elect its officers and set local policy.

The way to become a delegate to one of these conferences is through your own students' union. You will have to be elected by the students at your university to represent their views. You will also have had to spend some time in student politics so you can effectively get round the political jargon and agenda bandied about at conferences at this level. However, it is extremely useful experience for confident people interested in debating student issues at a national level.

## Lifesavers⊗

The help for this area of student life will be provided within your university, either by your students' union or your department.

Information about what is in the area outside the campus is in local phone books and libraries.

Go to your students' union to see what it offers. If you are interested in getting involved at a national level then contact the NUS or your NUS regional office.

The National Union of Students, Mandela House, 461 Holloway Road, London N7 6LJ, tel 071-272 8900.

NUS Northern Ireland, 34 Botanic Avenue, Belfast BT7 1JQ, tel 0232 244641.

NUS Scotland, 11 Broughton Market, Edinburgh EH1 3PP, tel 031-556 6598.

UCMC/NUS Wales, 107 Walter Road, Swansea SA1 5QQ, tel 0792 643323.

NUS North East, c/o Teesside University Student Union, Borough Road, Middlesbrough TS1 3BA, tel 0642 249079.

NUS North West, c/o University of Lancaster Student Union, Bowland Annexe, Lancaster LA1 4YT, tel 0524 35638.

NUS East Midlands, c/o Loughborough Student Union, Ashby Road, Loughborough LE11 3TT, tel 0509 239754.

NUS West Midlands, c/o University of Birmingham Student Union, Edgbaston Park Road, Birmingham B15 2TU, tel 021-472 1625.

NUS East Anglia, c/o Hertfordshire University Student Union, PO Box 109, Hatfield AL10 9AB, tel 0707 272207.

NUS London, c/o ULU, Malet Street, London WC1E 7HY, tel 071-637 1181.

NUS South West, c/o University of Bristol Student Union, Queen's Road, Clifton, Bristol BS8 1LN, tel 0272 734970.

NUS South East, c/o University of Surrey Student Union, Guildford, Surrey GU2 5XH, tel 0483 575189.

# 5 Down to Work

One of the biggest adjustments to make when you get to university is the change in study techniques. You may well have come from a school where you were a big fish in a small pond, but when you get to university you will definitely be a small fish in a very big pond. You will be left largely to your own devices. There will be no one chasing you for essays, telling you which chapters are relevant or dictating course notes to you.

At some point during your university career you have to make a decision about what sort of degree you want. University is not only about the piece of paper you emerge with. Most people can get a 2:1 or a 2:2 without knocking themselves out and leave themselves time to do other things.

*Union President, University of London*

Studying effectively is all about organising yourself. The key is finding out everything possible about your course; the forms of assessment, when you will be examined and what you will be expected to have achieved at certain times during the year. Once you have this basic information, it will be much easier to organise yourself each week.

Other people's courses always seem better than your own because you don't have to do the work involved, so can appreciate the interest value.

*Fourth-year student, Edinburgh University*

# Types of course

## Traditional courses

Many people choose to follow a traditional course where they are expected to follow certain core subjects but will be able to choose a few options, usually in the second year, that allow them to study subject areas of special interest.

I did a traditional physics course and definitely think this is the best way to study physics at university. I don't believe I would have such a thorough knowledge of my subject had I done a modular degree where study and assessment are not cumulative. I acquired an increasing depth of knowledge as I progressed through the course.

*Graduate, Oxford University*

Traditional courses tend to be heavily weighted towards examination performance. However, you may be given the option, or might even be required, to submit an extended essay as well as, or instead of, a final exam paper. You may also be asked to do several pieces of assessed work throughout your course which will count as a small percentage of your final degree mark.

I feel that my dissertation was the most valuable thing I ever did at university. I was able to choose an unusual subject which really interested me and enjoyed having the time to go into the topic in detail. I also feel that this teaches you some very valuable skills. It is always useful to know how to

research a subject in depth and present it in
an interesting and readable form.

*Graduate, University of London*

Choosing to do a long essay can have certain advantages
in that it will mean that you have fewer finals papers to sit
– a definite blessing when it comes to facing a mound of
revision – and will give you the chance to study a topic in
considerable depth. However, long essays or dissertations
tend to be more time-consuming than revising. Your
decision should be made on the basis of whether you are
someone who performs well in exams or whether you do
better given time to work on something in more detail.

### Modular courses

Modular courses, where you choose a number of topics in
a range of areas to make up your degree, have always been
offered as part of the degrees run by the former polytech-
nics and colleges of higher education. They are now also
becoming increasingly available in traditional universities.

The only problem with my course is that I
would sometimes like to get more of a
chance to specialise. I have to do eight units
a year and feel as though this is too
disparate. I do like being able to choose what
I study though, rather than following a
course some woolly academic who studied
30 years ago has decided is useful for me to
know.

*Third-year student, Loughborough University*

Make sure you have as much information as possible
about the guidelines which govern how you choose your
options, as the way courses are run varies considerably
between different institutions. The best way to judge

which options you should take is to do those courses you think you are going to enjoy most. Don't feel pressurised into taking courses because you think you ought to: you are much more likely to do well if you enjoy the subject. However, you may have to have reached a certain standard before you are allowed to take a course. It is no good selecting an option which requires you to have studied French to A-level if the only time you have spoken French is on holiday when you were six.

My tip is to stick to whole units unless there is a course you especially want to study which is only run as a half unit. Remember, there is definitely more work involved in doing two half units than doing one whole unit. Lecturers treat half units as full unit courses and expect you to do as much preparation for the classes. I had to write six assessed essays for my full unit and ten for my two half units.

*Union President, University of London*

You may also be expected to take certain core units which you will have to pass before you are awarded your degree. If you don't like these courses, then remember you only have to pass, and don't knock yourself out trying to get top marks.

University departments are usually very good at supplying all the information students need to make their decisions. Make sure you read everything carefully and ask your tutor for help. You can set up an agreement with your tutor to lay out what you should be doing.

On a modular course you are assessed throughout your time at university. Your coursework and examinations are taken into account, although certain courses and years may be given more weighting than others. Modular degree students have an advantage over traditional course students in that they have a good idea of what degree they are likely to get before they sit their final exams.

> I fully recommend modular degrees. I was able to get a physics and English degree which would have been impossible under a traditional system. Their great advantage is their flexibility. Many people find their interests change during their time at university and a modular degree can reflect this.

*Graduate, University of London*

Bear in mind that you will have to be well organised when following a modular degree, as you cannot be late handing in essays. Your essays have to be consistently good and your attendance at lectures, seminars and tutorials is often part of your assessment. Ask for advice from your tutors and take your time when choosing options.

### Placement courses

Some courses require you to undertake a short work placement or an exchange which is not directly assessed but is intended to give you an idea of how your degree can be used in the outside world. These are usually arranged at the beginning of your second year. Your tutors will give you information about firms that offer such placements or help you arrange your own.

> We were really lucky because our course also attracted a lot of industrial competitions where local firms would approach us for ideas and then pay the students whose ideas they used. In the project I was involved in, we were given the opportunity to have

something made up from the fabric design they had used. I have this really great bag made from our design. It is also a good way of supplementing the grant.

*Undergraduate, now Welfare Officer, Loughborough University*

## Sandwich courses

Sandwich courses usually involve doing a year's work placement in an industry connected with your degree after your second year. You can make other arrangements, such as working for the four summer terms or holidays. The placement is regarded as a full-time job and you may be paid a very good wage. On the other hand, you may not be so lucky, and may end up being used as cheap labour. Talk to your tutors about the reputation of the firm you will be working for. They will also be able to suggest who to approach for sandwich experience. If you are a sponsored student then you will probably do your placement with the firm that is sponsoring you.

**Note that you will not receive your maintenance grant while on placement.**

I was sent to the Gambia to look at the disease-carrying properties of insects. When I got back I realised this was something I wanted to pursue and it is the area I am now doing my PhD in. This does cause some strange reactions at parties – for some reason people don't expect a woman to be studying mosquito guts. However, it was really useful when I took my finals as there was a question that we hadn't really covered in our lectures and I was able to bring in what I had learnt in my sandwich year.

*Postgraduate, Salford University*

Your work will be assessed while you are on placement and your employer will be asked for a written report on your performance. You will then have to do a detailed project which will be assessed as part of your final degree mark.

Sandwich years give you valuable work experience and may enable you to clear some of your debts at the same time. However, some students who have signed up for sandwich courses cannot find placements. If this happens to you then get in touch with your department. They will try to help you or make arrangements for you to go straight into your final year. You may need help adjusting to the disappointment of not getting a placement and completing your finals without the support of your peers. Your students' union and department will be able to provide counselling.

### Part-time courses

Many students follow degree courses on a part-time basis. You will usually be offered a choice of following an evening course or joining the undergraduate courses during the day. You will have to be prepared to do a lot of organisation yourself, but studying in this way can be a good option for people who have outside commitments, or those who are returning to education after a break.

Unfortunately, as a part-time student you will not receive a mandatory (maintenance or fees) grant unless you are on an initial teacher-training course. Other courses, such as further teacher-training and other professional courses, are eligible for discretionary grants, however, and you can also get student loans for many part-time courses.

I find that the amount of time I have to spend travelling in to university is prohibitive. I don't even really get time to use the library properly because it takes me four hours to travel for two hours of seminars.

*First-year student, Kent University*

You should keep your department informed of your needs, especially if you have problems organising your timetable. You may be able to make special arrangements with the library whereby they will let you have books out for a bit longer if they know you are only coming into college once or twice a week.

One of the problems I found was that, as a part-time student, I ended up choosing my courses around what the department was offering at the times when I could actually travel in to the department.

*First-year student, University of Sussex*

## Courses in Scotland and Northern Ireland

### Scotland

The courses in Scotland are generally very much more flexible. You can change courses during the time you are at university. It is one of the many things which make us special.

*Fourth-year student, Edinburgh University*

Courses in Scotland are structured differently to those in England, Wales and Northern Ireland and last for four years. The first year is spent studying your main subject together with one closely related to it and a subject of your own choice which can be completely unrelated to your main subject. This year is generally regarded as making up for the difference in academic standard between English A-levels and Scottish Highers. English students with particularly good A-levels are sometimes exempt from this year. More usually though, they are encouraged to spend the year studying subjects which are completely unrelated to the degree they want to take.

I took a really basic course designed for arts students because, as a maths and physics student, my tutor told me it was foolproof. 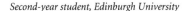 He was wrong. Unfortunately the examiners didn't share my sense of humour and failed me. I can continue with my degree but I might have a problem when I get to the end of my fourth year because I might not have enough courses. I don't know what will happen to my grant at that point.

*Second-year student, Edinburgh University*

The Scottish degree structure means you get the chance to study various subjects you are interested in before making your final decision. Some Scottish universities now run modular degrees which allow an even greater level of flexibility.

My sister came here intending to study for a business degree. She took linguistics as her third subject in the first two years. When it came to making her final choice, she decided that she was more interested in linguistics than business studies and took that as her final degree. Because of the flexibility of Scottish degrees she was able to completely alter her degree without repeating any years.

*President of the Students' Association, Edinburgh University*

## Northern Ireland

The Irish education system is completely compatible with the English and Welsh systems. The two universities in Northern Ireland – Queen's in Belfast, and Ulster – offer a wide range of undergraduate and postgraduate degree courses and have a very good reputation.

The only difference I think there is between Irish and English universities is that there is a greater political heritage in Ireland. The history courses, for instance, will have a greater political element. However, it is possible to stay out of politics altogether if that is what you want although, obviously, there are lots of political platforms if you enjoy the debates and involvement.

*Welfare Officer, Queen's University Belfast*

# Studying abroad

Increasingly students are being offered the opportunity to spend some time studying abroad, and not just as a requirement of language courses. With the introduction of the European single market, many universities recognise the importance of wider European knowledge and are incorporating language or overseas study into their courses.

Some of the people on my textile course were able to arrange to spend a term at a European university instead of arranging a work placement. Work placements are normally only for two weeks but the college was quite happy to let people go abroad for a term because they were continuing their studies.

*Welfare Officer, Loughborough University*

Your university may run schemes you can apply for and there are also national schemes such as ERASMUS and TEMPUS which help students to meet the costs of living and studying abroad. Full details can be found in *Studying Abroad* published by Hobsons, and from your university.

If you are taking a language degree then you will usually be offered the choice of travelling abroad to attend a university or teach in a school as an assistant. You should speak to your department, which will help you make all the arrangements.

The year I spent in Spain was definitely the best year of my life. I was left to arrange my own timetable with the university, although it was recommended that I should attend at least ten hours of lectures a week. I did this for the first three weeks but, as nobody seemed particularly bothered whether I was there or not, by the time I left I was going for about two hours. The rest of the time was my own.

*Graduate, University of London*

# Teaching methods

### Lectures

Teaching in universities is far less personal than the tuition you will have received at school. You will have to rely on your own initiative to a greater extent and be prepared to collate your own information.

If you are an arts student much of your course will be covered by lectures. These are talks given by tutors to a large (between about 50 and 100) group of students. You will be expected to take your own notes and may have to sign an attendance list to prove you were there. There will rarely be an opportunity for discussion and debate in lectures.

Personally I found lectures very useful. I went to all of mine and only missed six in three years, so I had the whole course covered. My notes were what I then used to revise from.

*Union President, University of London*

Some people find it particularly difficult to adjust to this form of teaching. Any reading you can do in advance will help you get over the feeling of being completely lost in a sea of unfamiliar faces and subjects. Your lecture subjects will be posted on departmental notice-boards.

I didn't like lectures. Only two of my courses had lectures which were directly relevant. With the other courses, very few lectures covered the texts I was studying. I found it more useful to use the time to gather information about the books I was going to need to prepare for examination.

*Graduate, University of London*

Some examinations will be based on what has been covered in your lectures. Find out if this is the case in your department as you will have to make sure you take a comprehensive set of notes to help you with your revision.

There is definitely an art attached to learning how to take notes, and everybody develops his or her own style. General tips, though, are to write down key ideas rather than whole sentences, leave lots of space on the paper so that you have room to add things later and use headings as you take notes to give them some structure. It is probably unrealistic to think you will be able to go through your notes after each lecture and turn them into beautifully crafted pieces of English. Just make sure you have the key points down in a way you will be able to understand later.

## Fieldwork and laboratory work

If you are studying a non-humanities subject then a large part of your course will be taught through laboratory and/or fieldwork. You will have more timetabled hours than humanities students and will spend a great deal of your time in laboratories. You will also have to work on your own initiative to a greater extent, taking responsibility for your experiments.

If fieldwork is a requirement of your course then you will be expected to go on at least two or three major field expeditions. These will occur during the vacations, so you may find that your holiday or earning plans have to be delayed. You will have to undertake a fieldwork project under your own initiative for your final degree result. Your department will usually offer several alternatives which you can sign up for, or you can arrange your own project with your tutor. Fieldwork is usually carried out in pairs and you may not always get the choice of who your partner is.

We spent six weeks living in a caravan in Iona mapping an area of rocks. Not an obvious recipe for fun, but we had such a good time only one of us managed to complete our final-year project. This could also have had something to do with the fact that we were the only pair in our department to take a TV with us, and insist that a television cable was laid from the nearest farmhouse to our caravan.

*Graduate, Aberystwyth University*

## Seminars

Seminars are discussions between a smaller group of students, with a tutor present to guide the proceedings. They can be extremely useful sessions, particularly if the group is vocal and forthcoming with its ideas. They are an increasingly common way of teaching.

I remember my seminars in my first year. There was this one guy who was a big drama queen and very fond of the sound of his own voice. The thing was that he repeated the same point the tutor had just made but took three times as long and made it twice as complicated. The rest of the group ended up being very good at getting its points out very quickly.

*Third-year student, University of London*

You may be asked to write a paper for one of your seminars and present it to the class. The content of a seminar paper will be the same as that of an essay but you will have to present it in a different way. You should stick to the same structure as you would for an essay: an introduction, discussion broken down into short points and a conclusion, but remember that your audience will be listening to you rather than reading your essay. They won't be able to go back and read things they have missed so make your points clearly and concisely, linking them with a logical thread. Don't be daunted by speaking in front of your class, you will all have to do it at some point. Most students find this is a valuable experience.

Personally, two hours talking about Adam Smith didn't really turn me on but the tutor was totally passionate about the man, which

was great. I did my five-minute presentation
and he did the rest of the talking.

*Fourth-year student, Edinburgh University*

Do not write your notes on A4 paper as these will hide
your face and you won't hold the attention of the class.
Write notes on index cards, which are much easier to hold
and refer to. If you are nervous about speaking in front of
people and find that you shake, leaning on a table or a
chair can help. Remember to speak slowly, taking deep
breaths and, if you lose track of what you are saying, just
pause and gather your thoughts. If your mind goes completely blank, then ask someone in the group where you
had got to; this is also a good way of testing whether they
were listening!

I asked my tutor whether he thought the
younger undergraduates had found it
difficult to have me as a mature student in
the seminars, but he was very pleased that all
the seminars had lasted for the full two
hours. I just found I had to hold back on the
cynicism when we came round to discussing
life and death questions.

*First-year mature student, University of Sussex*

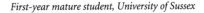

## Tutorials

Tutorials may be individual or small group discussions
with your tutor on specific subjects related to your
coursework. How often you are timetabled to meet with
your tutor varies in different institutions. Tutorials are
probably the most valuable periods of teaching time you
have, particularly if you get on well with your tutor.

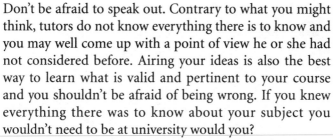

My tutorial partner and I would get together before our tutorial and work out the areas we had common difficulties with. This not only saved time but impressed the hell out of our tutor.

*Graduate, Oxford University*

Don't be afraid to speak out. Contrary to what you might think, tutors do not know everything there is to know and you may well come up with a point of view he or she had not considered before. Airing your ideas is also the best way to learn what is valid and pertinent to your course and you shouldn't be afraid of being wrong. If you knew everything there was to know about your subject you wouldn't need to be at university would you?

Your personal tutor is also the person you should talk to if you have any problems which might have repercussions for your studies. The earlier your department knows about any problems, the sooner it will be able to make any special arrangements to help you. You won't have to give any personal details – broad outlines will do – but there is nothing worse than being hounded for an essay when the whole world is crumbling around you, so let them know. If you really don't fancy talking to anyone in your department, then go to your students' union who will be able to act as mediators.

# Facilities and study skills

## Your fellow students

Whether or not you are assigned a tutorial partner, your fellow students are a valuable study aid. Comparing notes and talking about difficulties is very beneficial. It is much easier to solve a problem if there are several brains tackling it and you will get a broader idea of your course by comparing ideas. You can also form a pressure group with the other students if you are all unhappy with a particular lecturer or course.

Peer pressure is an odd phenomenon. Some students feel inadequate because they feel they will never be able to keep up with that perfect student who always gets essays in on time and is extremely vocal in class. Other people feel pressurised into appearing casual and dismissive about work.

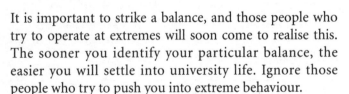 Different people have to do different amounts of work for the same results. Some people have to work very hard and others can sail through by doing very little. A lot of this will obviously depend on the course you are doing. History students, for instance, have what appears to be a justified reputation of doing very little work for their degree, whereas medics have ludicrous timetables. You just have to make sure you set yourself the right amount of study time for you and your course.

*Graduate, University of London*

It is important to strike a balance, and those people who try to operate at extremes will soon come to realise this. The sooner you identify your particular balance, the easier you will settle into university life. Ignore those people who try to push you into extreme behaviour.

### Time management

First of all, check to see whether your university has a study skills induction module. These are increasingly common and extremely useful.

The important thing to remember is that no one expects you to work all the time. If you did nothing but study, you would miss the very important opportunity university offers you to develop as a person. Time management is a phrase you will become very familiar with during your time at university: it is the key to making sure you can fit everything in.

University is about the whole life experience, not just about getting a piece of paper at the end of three or four years.

*Welfare Officer, Aberystwyth University*

The first thing to do is to work out your timetable and make a clear copy. It is remarkable how much easier things become once you know where you are supposed to be and when. You should then sit down and work out which courses require you to do background reading or preparation and which tutors want essays from you. Plan your weekly work schedule round this information.

Don't set yourself unrealistic work schedules – this will only depress you when you fail to keep up with them – and don't work for excessively long periods of time. How long you find you can concentrate is up to you to discover, but a general guideline is to try working for 40 minutes and relaxing for ten or 20 minutes. When you do stop, don't feel guilty and make sure you relax properly. Have a cup of coffee, read the papers or flop in front of the television for a while.

You may find it useful to make lists of what you have to do by certain dates: it is very therapeutic to cross things off a list once you have completed them. You can order these lists into 'urgent' tasks, 'necessary' tasks and those which can be left until last. If you find that your list is heavily weighted on the 'urgent' side then you are not planning your time well. Reorganise things to give yourself more realistic time schedules.

If you find you have particular difficulties organising your workload then try keeping a diary for a week. Write down everything you do during the day, honestly, and then look back on it and see where you have wasted time, where you have used time efficiently and where you felt you needed to relax more. You can then rearrange your schedule around this information.

Where you choose to work is very much an individual decision. Some people like working in a library environment where everything is quiet and books are easily accessible. Other people feel happier working in a more relaxed situation. Decide where you work best and then go there for your planned study periods.

## Studying as a mature student

Some universities have a high proportion of mature students following degree courses and run special induction courses to help mature students fit back into the higher education system. These will include sessions on essay writing and study techniques, as well as the usual undergraduate induction information.

I find that mature students tend to be more motivated. I have to be because I have less time to study than other undergraduates, as my three children still need looking after. The thing that they didn't tell you at the induction day was that you were going to have to give seminar presentations to ten 20 year-olds. Mind you, this wasn't a problem after the first few occasions. You just have to be very selective about what you do and what you don't do.

*First-year student, University of Sussex*

## The library

You are likely to spend quite a few of your university days in the library so it is obviously very important to learn where the library is and how to use it effectively.

There are several things you will need to familiarise yourself with in the library, but first, you will have to learn how the classification system works. Books are usually classified by subject matter but you will be given instructions on how the system in your university operates.

The photocopier is the most useful piece of library equipment for you to get to know. The photocopiers in university are very much cheaper than photocopiers in commercial print shops. The savings are worth the back-breaking process of standing bent double while you churn out chunks of text books and friends' essays. Do be aware, though, of copyright law: it is illegal to copy more than a small amount from any one book. Check with your librarian before you copy anything from a book – published or not. Beware, too, of plagiarism: if your department suspects you of copying from a book or from another student, you are in danger of losing your degree.

Learning how to use the various computerised systems is also very useful. You can find out whether a book you want is stocked in the library by using microfiche files. Some libraries now have on-line cataloguing systems which can tell you whether a book is available or not. Don't be scared off by technology, as it is all extremely user-friendly.

One of the lessons new students need to learn really quickly is that it is essential to go and get any references given during a lecture or tutorial immediately. If you don't go to the library for a couple of days then everyone else on the course will have been there before and it will be a case of "Wot, no books!"

*Union President, University of London*

You can get a good idea of what is expected from you by looking at past papers, which the library or your department will stock. Some large universities will have a special 'past papers' department. The library will also house past students' dissertations and theses which you may need to use as sources of information for your research. Remember to credit the author; copyright law applies as much to other students' past work as it does to books.

Audio-visual material is being used increasingly in higher education as access to video recorders widens, and many libraries now run video rental services as well. The rules are likely to be different from those governing books so check before you borrow a video when it has to be returned; bringing it back the following day may not be possible if you have to travel halfway across town to a video machine.

You should also remember that you are not just restricted to your university library. You can join any local library providing you take proof of your local address. You might find there is less competition for recommended books at a public library.

### Technology labs

Your university will probably offer access to computer terminals for technology needs. If you need to use a computer as part of your course, then you will be given tuition. Even if you can't see what use a computer could be to a language or English course, you may be surprised. Some work may need to be handed in word-processed and it is very much cheaper if you can do this yourself. Knowing your way around a computer is a very useful skill to have anyway, regardless of whether or not your course requires it. Check to see if the university offers tutorial or seminar sessions.

## Assessment and exams

### Passing exams

However your course is structured, you are unlikely to be able to escape exams altogether. The important thing to remember about sitting exams is that it is the first 50 per cent that really matters. Anything above that is a bonus. You will not be let into university if you are not capable of getting 50 per cent in an exam so, providing you do enough work and give yourself time to revise, there is no need to panic.

How well you do in an exam can be divided into one quarter how good you are at the subject, one quarter how hard you work, one quarter your exam technique and one quarter luck.

*Union President, University of London*

Once in the exam make sure you know what format the paper will take, READ THE INSTRUCTIONS at the top to check, and follow them carefully. Always attempt to answer all the questions you are supposed to; it is much easier to get marks by attempting to answer a new question than by continuing with one you have already answered.

Timing your exam papers is very important. You should always allow time to plan your answers and read them through afterwards. This might sound like a luxury you can ill afford but it is amazing how many careless mistakes slip through when you are writing at speed.

If your exam is going to be judged largely on essays, you will probably find it helpful to do several timed essays as practice. These are not only good revision aids but will give you an idea of how much you can write in the time. The more you do, the easier it will become to answer questions well within the time.

## How to revise

The amount of revision you get done is in inverse proportion to the number of books you have in front of you. It is much better to find two or three books which contain key information and read them well than to read the introductions to a whole mound of books.

*Union President, University of London*

For essay-based subjects you should aim to be in a position where you have covered the range of possible topics for the questions. The main difference between arriving at this position at university and at school is that you will have to gather most of the information you need yourself. It takes quite a long time to collate your notes, reading and essays and you will find that the photocopier becomes your best friend as the exams approach. You should also consider swapping essays with others on your course as this is a great way of covering many topics relatively painlessly. It's a good idea to leave yourself about a month to concentrate on learning the information you have gathered.

For practical-based subjects you should make sure that you have completed all your assessed projects by the time you are examined. If you have to carry out a project or experiment under examination conditions then always double check your equipment to see if it is all there and working.

### A healthy body and an active mind

The usual rules about keeping healthy are even more important to follow when preparing for exams. Make sure you allow yourself time off, eat a healthy diet and get outside at least once a day. A recent study has shown a remarkable and close correlation between aerobic exercise and academic ability. The subjects' intellectual abilities were tested before, and immediately after, they had taken aerobic exercise and all showed a marked improvement. You may want to consider spending time in the gym or jogging as exams approach, even if you do revert to being a couch potato the moment they are over.

Everyone is different, but unless you have an astonishing constitution, do not stay up the night before an exam. It might seem like the end of the world if you don't read up on that topic just once more but a tired brain acts in strange ways. You will often end up squeezing out the information you have absorbed by trying to cram at the last minute. Even if you have done very little work, you are better off sitting an exam with a refreshed brain. Exams are largely assessed on your response to the question. A tired brain cannot respond very effectively.

## What happens if you fail?

How seriously your university regards failing a course will vary from place to place. Most departments will offer you a resit or allow you to retake a year, but some universities will throw you off the course. If there are any reasons why you have failed your exams, other than not doing enough work, then let your tutors know as soon as possible. If there are any medical reasons for you not doing well, then get a medical certificate from your doctor, preferably before you take the exam.

You may have to pay to take resits and they are often scheduled during those precious summer holidays or on the day college re-opens after them. These are all things you should consider seriously before deciding you don't have to bother revising because your particular university will allow you to resit exams.

Even if you think you are going to fail your exams you should still sit them. If you don't sit your exams then you will definitely lose your entitlement to a grant. If you take your exams and fail them, you still leave the option open of appealing to your local education authority for a discretionary grant.

Your students' union can act as a mediator between you, your department and your local education authority in this situation, so contact them as soon as you find yourself in this position.

## Academic appeals

Most universities have a formal structure through which you can appeal if you feel you have been unfairly treated in any aspect of your academic teaching or assessment. You should talk to your students' union and your tutors about what form appeals take at your college. Make sure you collect all the information you feel is relevant, particularly if there are good reasons why you have not done well.

You may also be asked to attend an academic appeal if your tutors or examiners have cause to question your academic performance because they feel you have been cheating or you have plagiarised someone else's work. These can be very formal affairs and you may be entitled to legal representation. Get advice from your students' union.

If you have to retake a year you won't be given a grant unless you can prove that there were medical reasons for having to do so. It is possible that your university will allow you to sit exams again at the end of the year but you may be banned from attending lectures and classes for that year.

## Changing course

I changed from French and drama to Hispanic studies at the end of my first year because I wasn't enjoying the course, the place or the people. Because the transfer was within the same college, all I had to do was send the letter my tutor wrote outlining the academic reasons for my changing course to my LEA and they gave me a grant to cover the whole of my new course. I am much happier with my new course and very glad that I changed.

*Fourth-year student, University of London*

Many students get to university and decide that they have chosen the wrong course or even the wrong place. You won't usually have too many problems if you want to change course within the same institution, unless that course is already oversubscribed.

Grant-wise, you have to make a decision before you have been on your course for seven weeks into your second term of your first year. If you change before this point then you will receive funding for your new course. You will need your tutor to endorse the change and the transfer of your grant.

If you change at any point after this date then you will need your tutor to approve your transfer on academic and educational grounds and it will then be left to the discretion of your education authority whether they fund your new course. Most LEAs are quite good about this providing you have the necessary letter from your tutor.

If you want to change universities then you will need two letters; one confirming you have a place at the new university and another from your tutor approving the transfer on educational grounds.

After an unsuccessful attempt at a law degree, I decided it was time to change. Law did not retain my interest or concentration for long enough to tempt me away from the new-found pleasures of undergraduate life. I failed my first-year exams – badly. My tutor told me I could sit the exams again in a year's time but could not attend the lectures and tutorial in the meantime. I also lost my entitlement to a grant for that year. The year passed. I took a number of temporary jobs and tried to complete an intensive, and expensive, legal correspondence course but all to no avail. I did only slightly better than the previous year. I accepted a place at the same university to do history. I thought I had ruined my chances of getting a grant for the whole three years but after my parents had paid £8,000 fees and living expenses for the first year my LEA generously paid the full whack for the rest of my course.

*Graduate, University of London*

# Lifesavers⊗

## Organisations

If you experience any academic difficulties you can speak to your course representative, your personal tutor or another lecturer with whom you get on, or your students' union which can act as a mediator between you and the university.

## Publications

*Higher Education in the European Community* lists grants for students wanting to study in the Community. Published by the Publications Office, 5 rue de Commerce, BP 1003, 2985 Luxembourg. You can also purchase it from HMSO and in bookshops at £11.95.

*Scholarships Abroad* is published annually and lists scholarships and bursaries which British students who want to study abroad can apply for. You need to have been given a place at a university abroad and most grants are given for postgraduate study. Published by the British Council, 65 Davies Street, London W1Y 2AA, tel 071-930 8466.

*Study Abroad* lists over 200,000 scholarships, awards and prizes in universities throughout the world. Published by UNESCO, 7 Place de Fontenoy, 75700 Paris, France, or available from HMSO or bookshops at £12.50.

*Studying in Europe,* published by Hobsons Publishing PLC.

# 6 Health and Welfare

## General health

It may not seem like your most pressing task when you arrive at your new university, but registering with a doctor is vital and should be done AS SOON AS POSSIBLE. It is all too easy to get caught up with sorting out your timetable and the hectic social activity of freshers' week, but it is precisely during this time you might have cause to regret not registering with a doctor.

You should not be worried about registering with a different practice to the one you have been going to for years. You will be able to return to your home GP in the holidays as a visitor, but this is no good if you are ill during term time. You do need to register with a doctor in your university town because this is where you will be spending at least 33 weeks of the year.

> It took me ages to register with my doctor. I only went after my pigeonhole had become completely jammed with reminders from the medical centre. This was really stupid as it only took ten minutes and I was really lucky because about a month afterwards I became quite ill and needed a prescription. I certainly wasn't in any state to sort out registering at that stage of the game.

*First-year student, University of London*

Your university will have a doctor either on site or a practice close by which it recommends. You will be given details in the first few days. You do not have to register with the college doctor if you don't want to, but it is a good idea to register with a surgery within a mile's radius of where you live. This way you will be entitled to home visits should you need them. Details of doctors can be found in the local library or post office or obtained from the Family Practitioners' Committee.

Wherever you decide to register you will need to take your medical card with you, even if your college has asked you to bring a medical form from your previous doctor. If you have lost your medical card then go to a local surgery and fill in an application for a new one.

You must also remember to register with a dentist as well. You may have to try several before you find one that is not oversubscribed. Some hospitals do provide emergency treatment but this is not a method you should rely on.

## Medical charges

Students under 19 are entitled to free medical treatment. This includes prescription charges, sight tests and dental treatment. Once you pass your 19th birthday you will have to go through the mound of paperwork that is involved in proving that you are on a low income, and the student grant certainly qualifies! It is a good idea to tackle this well in advance, particularly if you need medication on a regular basis, as it can take a month or longer for your claim to be assessed. You can get the relevant forms and leaflets which explain the benefits, refunds and help you are entitled to, and how to claim, from the local DSS office or by writing to the Agency Benefits Office, DSS, Sandyford House, Newcastle upon Tyne NE2 1AA.

## Stress

For many students, moving to university will be the first time they take sole responsibility for their lifestyle and health. It is very important that you look after your health. If you are ill you will not be able to participate fully in university life.

DON'T SKIP MEALS: your body needs regular food to be able to cope with the stresses of moving, starting your course and making new friends. You should also make sure you get as much sleep as you need. Different people need varying amounts of sleep so don't feel pressurised into staying up all night if you can't function without your eight hours a night.

Stress is very high among students when they first move to university because they have to deal with a lot of changes all at once. There are various relaxation techniques that can help you reduce stress, which your GP will be able to advise you on. One of the best ways of relieving stress is by taking exercise. This has great general health benefits too. It is important that you don't forget about keeping fit when you get to university. If you are living in hall close to your department and the students' union, it is very easy to do absolutely no exercise. If you find yourself slipping into this situation and do not fancy playing any sports, you should at least make a concerted effort to walk or cycle into town rather than take public transport all the time.

## Alternative therapies

If you are not happy with conventional medicine then you should talk to your doctor about the alternatives. Many doctors have a positive attitude and will be happy to discuss the options. The NHS now recognises the benefits of homeopathic medicine, which uses natural herbs and products to treat ailments. Other practices such as acupuncture and osteopathy are also recognised as being beneficial.

There is always a danger, however, particularly when you are feeling ill and vulnerable, that you will be more easily persuaded into believing in some apparently magical cure. Stick to alternatives which already have an established reputation, talk to your doctor and use alternative remedies in conjunction with traditional practices.

# Eating disorders

I am seeing an increasing number of
students, both male and female, suffering
from eating disorders, which is extremely
worrying.

*Welfare Officer, Aberystwyth University*

Many people don't realise they are suffering from an
eating disorder, as problems with food take many forms
and have a variety of underlying psychological causes.
The anxieties brought on by the stress of starting at university can sometimes manifest themselves as eating
disorders.

There are three main types of eating disorder. They are known as anorexia nervosa, when people consistently don't eat as much as they need; bulimia, which is a cycle of binge eating followed by starvation or other forms of purging such as making yourself sick after eating, and compulsive eating. In the United States bulimia is so common among young women college students it is known as the 'college girl disease'.

Doctors are now very aware of the devastating effects of eating disorders and are sympathetic when approached for treatment. It is very important you seek expert advice if you feel you are having problems with food and there is a network of organisations around the country that will be able to give you such help.

I suffered from bulimia for most of my adolescence and still had the disease when I came to college. My course was very demanding and I continued to suffer from bulimia throughout my second year. However, as my confidence increased and, helped by my boyfriend, I was able to begin to recover in the third year. I am still not completely cured but am very much better than when I first came to college.

*Fourth-year student, University of London*

## Sexually transmitted diseases

University is a time when many people have sex for the first time. You should be aware of the health risks an active sex life brings and know how to protect yourself (see the safe sex guidelines in the Safer sex section, page 166). Sexually transmitted diseases (STDs) can spread quickly in a community that is not aware of the implications of commencing sexual relationships.

There are a great number of sexually transmitted diseases and they can be spread between both men and women through contact with the genitals, mouth or fingers. The effects are varied. Some STDs cause only temporary discomfort but others can bring lasting damage to your health. Some of the symptoms take time to develop, so if you think you have been exposed to any kind of risk do not have sex again until you have been checked out by your doctor or a specialist clinic. You can get a list of local clinics from the phone book under venereal diseases or sexually transmitted diseases.

## Some signs of STD infection

➡ unusually coloured discharge or leakage from the penis
➡ unusual discharge from the vagina in terms of colour, odour or viscosity, possibly causing irritation
➡ sores or blisters around the penis, anus or vagina
➡ rash or irritation around the penis, anus or vagina
➡ a burning sensation or pain when you pee
➡ a need to pee more frequently
➡ pain when you have sex

You should not be embarrassed if you think you have a sexually transmitted disease as it is no reflection on you as a person. It can happen to anyone who is sexually active. Regular check ups at your local STD clinic could reduce your chance of contracting and passing on STDs. Counselling is also available at these clinics if you are at all concerned.

## HIV and AIDS

The most life-threatening of all diseases that can be sexually transmitted is that caused by the HIV virus. This can develop into full-blown AIDS, for which there is no known cure.

The HIV virus is spreading faster among heterosexuals than any other section of society. HIV and AIDS can affect you, whoever you are. Always take precautions and if you have any doubts or questions then seek advice from the network of specialist organisations listed in local phone books.

HIV stands for Human Immunodeficiency Virus. Being HIV positive means that the body has produced antibodies to the virus and has become more susceptible to illness. If someone starts to show symptoms of certain illnesses he or she is then classified as having ARC (AIDS Related Complex). AIDS (Acquired Immune Deficiency Syndrome) is only diagnosed when a person shows signs of having a series of infections and cancers resulting from contracting the HIV virus.

The HIV virus is transmitted through blood, semen, male pre-ejaculatory fluids, vaginal fluids and breast milk. For a person to become infected these fluids have to pass directly into the bloodstream in sufficient quantities: the HIV virus does not survive for long outside the body. Once you realise this, it is easy to dismiss the scare-mongering stories touted in the press when the virus first received publicity. There is no risk of the HIV virus being spread through everyday social activities such as kissing, sharing crockery, cutlery or food, shaking hands, hugging, swimming in public pools, using public loos, sneezing or coughing.

### Living with HIV

So, there is no risk to you from everyday activities if you live with somebody who is HIV positive. If you are HIV positive you should just make sure to take care if you injure yourself and disinfect everything that has come into contact with your blood. You should have a doctor's appointment every six months to check that the disease has not progressed, but remember that you have a right to confidentiality. This includes any medical test you might be asked to take by the college or an employer: you are under no obligation to inform either of them.

## High risk activities

Any activity which involves the transfer of bodily fluids, such as blood, urine, semen and vaginal fluids, puts you and your partner at risk. Unprotected penetrative intercourse is therefore a high risk activity. Anal intercourse is particularly risky because the lining of the rectum is thinner than that of the vagina and can therefore be ruptured more easily.

If you have unprotected sex with an infected woman during the time of her period the risk of contracting the virus increases by a factor of three.

## Lower risk activities

Vaginal penetrative intercourse with a condom, and oral sex, are both lower risk activities. However, the AIDS virus can be transmitted during oral sex if you have cuts or sores in your mouth so it is safer to use a non-lubricated condom; you can even get flavoured condoms for this purpose.

## Safe activities

Kissing carries no risk providing neither of you has cuts and sores in your mouth. Massage, mutual masturbation, sharing a shower and sharing sex toys, providing they are washed before your partner uses them, are all safe activities.

## How to protect yourself

Remember you only have to have sex with an infected partner ONCE to contract AIDS so it is vital that you protect yourself and your partner. If somebody tries to persuade you it isn't necessary to use a condom just point out they are risking their health as well as yours and REFUSE to sleep with them.

You cannot tell by looking at someone whether they are infected or not and the risk does not diminish the more times you sleep with them. So for the sake of your health and that of your partner always play safe.

LIBRARY
BISHOP BURTON COLLEG
BEVERLEY HU17 8QG

### To take an AIDS test or not

This is a choice only you can make and if you think there is a possibility that you have contracted the HIV virus, then you should go for counselling before you make the decision. Any of the STD clinics listed in the phone book will have specialist counsellors who will be happy to talk to you.

You may want to consider having an AIDS test before you enter a long-term relationship if you and your partner do not want to continue using condoms. However, on a note of caution, you have to be sure that you and your partner will not have unprotected sex outside the relationship. Don't believe anybody who says they have an AIDS test before each new relationship unless they provide some kind of proof.

# Preventive medicine

### Men's health

While women have known for years that they should regularly examine their breasts, men have not been so aware that they should examine their scrotums. Yet this is very important, as testicular cancer is most frequently found in young men in the 20–40 age group. If you do find any lumps or changes you should go immediately to your doctor. Any lumps are most likely to be harmless but should be checked out, not least for your peace of mind.

### Women's health

Many women prefer to be seen by a female doctor. You have the right to choose, so if your practice does not have a woman registered with it, ask for a list of Well women clinics or practices with registered women doctors available in the area. You may also want to get more information from a book called *Our Bodies, Ourselves* which is written by women and published by Penguin.

### Toxic Shock Syndrome (TSS)

TSS is believed to be caused by using tampons. Typical symptoms are quite similar to the 'flu' virus followed by diarrhoea, high temperature, vomiting, skin rashes on hands and feet, double vision and hair loss. These symptoms develop quickly and must be treated immediately, as women can die from TSS. Tampon manufacturers are increasingly recognising the potential dangers of tampon use and should be including more detailed instructions on how to use them safely. If you do use tampons, make sure you use the correct absorbency and change them regularly. It is advisable not to use tampons overnight.

### Cervical smears

Cancer of the cervix can be cured if it is caught early enough. The tests are slightly uncomfortable but not painful and every woman should have a smear test once every three years. Your doctor will send you a letter when your smear test is due. If you don't get a letter then you should ask for an appointment. The test only takes about two minutes and is well worth undergoing for the protection of your health.

> I had a smear test because I changed from the cap to the pill. Within a year I had gone from a completely clear test to one which showed I had pre-cancerous cells. Because this was spotted in time I was declared fit after laser treatment. It was a very worrying time but I am extremely glad I followed my doctor's advice and had regular tests. I don't even want to think about what would have happened if I hadn't.

*Second-year student, University of London*

### Breast examinations

You should examine your breasts once every month, ideally just after your last period as this is when the breasts are smallest and any changes are more visible. Check particularly for any nipple secretions, changes in the nipple, lumps, dimples or swelling. Your doctor, Well woman clinic or family planning clinic will be able to show you how to examine yourself correctly. If you do notice any changes, do not panic as the vast majority are completely harmless, but do go to your doctor as soon as you can.

## Sex and sexuality

The first thing to remember is that there is no 'norm' to which you have to conform. Your own sexuality is up to you to define and you should not feel pressurised, either by peers or sexual partners, into doing anything you do not feel comfortable with. Learning what gives you pleasure and how to talk about this with a partner is all part of developing your sexuality.

I met my first really serious boyfriend at college. It was a completely different relationship to any I had been in before because we were so compatible – same interests, same course, same friends, even nearly the same classes. The relationship broke up after a year because we both realised that we needed diversity in our relationships. However, we are still friends and now have a much better idea of what we need from a partner. I am glad I was able to find this out about myself through that relationship.

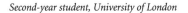

*Second-year student, University of London*

Many colleges are taking very positive steps to help gay, lesbian and bisexual students explore their sexuality. Your students' union should have a gay, lesbian and bisexual club which will provide you with a forum to meet other students who share your sexuality, arrange activities and provide you with any support you might need. If there is no such club at your university then you should ask your union how you can go about setting one up.

One of the things I found most useful when coming out was the lesbian, gay and bisexual support group at college; not as a place to meet potential partners but as a place to meet like-minded people and talk about my sexuality. I have found someone at college who I am extremely happy with. If you are open, honest and have a positive attitude to relationships, then college is the place where relationships can blossom. You establish yourselves as individuals without competing in peer groups. I probably would never have accepted my sexuality if I hadn't come to college. *'*

*Welfare Officer, Lampeter University*

Your welfare officer or student counsellor in the students' union can give you information and advice in complete confidence about any problem, regardless of your sexuality. The person who claims to have a trouble-free sex life the whole of the time is probably lying.

Sex is, and should be, fun and fulfilling. Don't let yourself be pressurised and don't put your health at risk.

## Safer sex

It is the responsibility of both sexual partners to practise safer sex. Be safe, not sorry.

We went round Bangor handing out free condoms to anyone over 14 and talking to them about safe sex practices. We wanted to talk to the 12–14 year-olds as well and thought we should give them something. We settled on chewing gum because it seemed as good an idea as anything else. Unfortunately Bangor is a small and very religious community and there were people who thought we definitely should not be walking round the streets handing out condoms. *'*

*Welfare Officer, Bangor University*

Safer sex is not only a way of preventing the spread of HIV and AIDS but can also open up new opportunities in the way you have intercourse. By exploring completely safe options, such as massage and kissing, you can find new ways of enjoying your partner's sexual company and giving each other pleasure.

## Contraception

I see a frightening number of first-year pregnancies. Many people still believe the old wives' tales such as you can't get pregnant the first time you have sex, or if you shower afterwards or get up and walk round. It makes me wonder what the sex education in schools is like.

*Women's Officer, Swansea University*

It is the responsibility of both partners to discuss contraception, and not only as a means of preventing unwanted pregnancy. The responsibility has often tended to fall on the shoulders of women because there is a greater range of contraception available to them. However, contraception is something that men should be prepared to discuss. It is much easier and much less traumatic to prevent a pregnancy than to terminate one. No contraceptive method is 100 per cent safe, and some do have side effects, so you should take time to find the method which suits you both and consider contraception and safer sex needs together.

You can get contraception from your GP practice if it has the letter C after its name. If it does not provide this service, your doctor will be able to give you the details of family planning clinics or Well women clinics in the area.

My boyfriend and I were each other's first sexual partners. After a few months of using condoms, we decided that I should take contraceptive advice from my college GP. Her attitude to students seemed disdainful: the pill was the only option available to a responsible young female (regardless of my physical condition or AIDS awareness), as condoms often fail and she had dealt with 15 prospective abortions that year. I decided to go elsewhere for advice. The family planning clinic is fantastic, as is my new doctor. It was definitely worth changing practice. I don't have to insist on explanations or alternatives and won't be intimidated into situations which don't suit me. Getting contraceptive advice doesn't have to be remotely distressing and it is definitely worth asking round for a recommendation.

*Second-year student, Wolverhampton University*

## Condoms

A condom is also known as a sheath, rubber or johnny and is a thin rubber cover placed on the erect penis. If used correctly the condom is about 95 per cent effective in preventing unwanted pregnancy and is the best method for protecting you from STDs and HIV. It is even more effective if you use it with a spermicide pessary or jelly. You should always use a water-based lubricant such as KY Jelly, because oil-based lubricants like Vaseline can damage the condom. Remember that pre-ejaculatory fluids carry as much risk of transmitting STDs as semen, and can contain sperm. Condoms have no side effects on your health.

Always use a kite-marked condom. Make sure you read the instructions and expiry date carefully. This may sound very obvious, but unless you use condoms properly you might as well not bother.

It's amazing how many people think condoms only last for a few days. It's a condom, not a yoghurt. They last for years but should not be used after the expiry date.

*Welfare Officer, Bangor University*

Always put a condom on when the penis is erect, making sure you squeeze the end of the condom while you unroll it. This will give the sperm somewhere to go. Withdraw the penis immediately after ejaculation, as a condom will slip off a penis that is getting smaller. As you remove it hold the condom firmly at the base so that no sperm can escape and tie a knot in it before throwing it away (preferably not down the loo as it can get blocked). Do not place the penis near the vagina again until all sperm have been washed off.

A female condom has recently been introduced onto the market. It is similar to the male condom, although obviously much larger, and provides the same protection against sexually transmitted diseases and AIDS. It is inserted into the vagina before sex. It provides the same protection as the male condom and also has no side effects on your health.

## Pessaries

These are spermicidal capsules inserted into the vagina before intercourse. They provide added protection when used with barrier methods of contraception such as condoms, caps and diaphragms. Women should use pessaries particularly during the most fertile period of their cycle.

## The pill

There are two main types of contraceptive pill. The combined pill contains progesterone and oestrogen which work together to prevent ovulation. The mini-pill contains only progesterone which alters the cervical mucus so that the sperm can't get through and changes the lining of the uterus so it doesn't accept the egg. Most pills are taken for 21 days and then left for seven days, during which time you will have a period, but you should follow the instructions on the packet carefully.

The varieties of pill differ in strength and will be given to you after consultation with your doctor or family planning clinic. You must be open with them so they can sort out which one is likely to suit you best. You should also be prepared to experiment until you find a make which suits you.

The pill has the highest success rate in preventing pregnancy, providing you take it as prescribed. However, there are certain circumstances which reduce its effectiveness, such as an upset stomach or if you are taking antibiotics. Ask what these are when taking contraceptive advice and consult your doctor or family planning clinic if you have unprotected sex under these circumstances.

Some women are lucky and find that the pill suits them immediately. Others suffer side effects, such as weight gain, depression and nausea and the pill has been linked to reduced fertility after long-term use. Some studies have associated long-term use with an increased risk of cancer, thrombosis and other potentially life-threatening diseases. The risk increases again if you are a smoker. Always take medical advice. The pill does not provide any protection against STDs or HIV so should be used in conjunction with safer sexual practices.

### The diaphragm or cap

This is a rubber device which is inserted into the vagina before intercourse to cover the cervix. It should be left there for six hours after sex. Its effectiveness depends on how you use it and it must be used with a spermicide. It also has to be fitted initially by your doctor or clinic and should be checked regularly with your contraceptive adviser or GP. It too does not provide any protection from STDs and HIV.

### Intra-uterine device (IUD) or coil

This is a plastic tubing coil that is inserted into the uterus by a doctor and prevents the egg from settling in the uterus. The coil can cause damage to the uterus which may affect future fertility and cause heavy periods. It is not always effective and can cause serious problems if you get pregnant.

### Sponge

A circular soft sponge which is inserted into the vagina 24 hours before sex. It is impregnated with a spermicide and must be left in the vagina for six hours after sex. It carries about a 25 per cent risk of pregnancy.

### Natural rhythm

The basic idea is that you avoid sex during a woman's most fertile time (12 to 16 days before her next period) but this is very difficult to calculate, as women's menstrual cycles can alter dramatically. It involves taking your temperature every day and drawing up charts and doing complicated calculations.  You also have to have a very regular cycle for this to be at all effective. The risk of pregnancy is very high.

## Withdrawal

With this method the man withdraws before ejaculation. This is also a VERY unreliable method of contraception, as sperm are often present in the pre-ejaculatory fluids. DO NOT believe the old myths about not being able to get pregnant unless a man reaches orgasm.

## The morning after pill

This should only ever be used in emergency circumstances and never as a regular form of contraception. Most doctors and clinics will only be prepared to prescribe it a limited number of times within a twelve-month period, usually no more than three. It contains a large dose of the normal contraceptive pill and must be taken no later than 72 hours after sex. It definitely cannot be taken twice in the same menstrual cycle and may make you feel very ill for a few days afterwards.

## Abstinence

Celibacy is the only 100 per cent effective method of contraception and is practised by many students. You should not feel pressurised into having sex until or unless you feel ready. This will be different for each person. The number of sexual partners you have is NOT a sign of your maturity: you do not need to have a sexual relationship to prove that you are an adult. Respect for your body and emotions shows greater maturity and you will know when it is right for you to sleep with someone.

# Pregnancy

Signs of pregnancy are missed periods, nausea, vomiting and breast tenderness. If you think you might be pregnant then have a pregnancy test once your period is overdue. These are available from your doctor, family planning clinic or in kit form from your local pharmacy.

If you choose to have an abortion you should remember that the earlier it is done the safer the operation. You can have an abortion through the NHS or through a private clinic. The NHS treatment is free but you may have to wait for up to eight weeks. Private treatment is quicker but you will have to pay. The date of pregnancy is calculated from the first day of your last period unless you are particularly irregular, but an examination by your doctor will give you a rough estimate. Abortions are usually carried out between seven and 12 weeks from your last period. If you suffer depression following your abortion you should seek expert advice from one of the specialist clinics listed in the local phone book.

Students in Northern Ireland still have to go to England for abortions and should contact the women's officer or welfare officer for details of how this can be arranged. We used to have a conditional pro-choice policy at Queen's but we now have both pro-life and pro-choice policies, which basically means we can distribute information. There are a growing number of students here who support the pro-choice argument. Ian Paisley came to speak at the opening of the Brook Centre here and we were able to shout him down which was great.

*Welfare Officer, Queen's University Belfast*

If you choose to continue with the pregnancy you should also seek specialist advice. You will have many choices to make throughout the pregnancy and birth and the more information you can gather, the better equipped you will be to make these decisions. It is also very important for both you and the baby that you attend antenatal clinics early and continue to do so throughout the pregnancy. There are lots of books and organisations which can provide you with the help you need.

Childcare provision in universities varies greatly around the country. If you need childcare you should make arrangements with your tutors and lecturers as soon as possible so they can help you organise your timetable to cover all your work. Your students' union is the first place to go to for information as it will also be able to tell you where you can go to find out about the extra benefits you can claim.

## Sexual assault

Sexual assault can take many forms. If you feel you have been forced into any sexual situation then you have been sexually assaulted. These situations can range from an uninvited kiss to rape.

Unfortunately there are some people who believe that because you have agreed to spend an evening in their company, you will automatically agree to sleep with them. This is wrong. You should not feel guilty or as though you have provoked an assault simply because you have allowed someone to buy you a beer.

Say NO firmly and don't be afraid to tell someone you feel as though they are sexually assaulting you: they should respect your right to refuse whatever the circumstances. This can sometimes get through the alcoholic fuzz and connect with the brain cells. If this does not work and the attack continues then report it as soon as possible.

You can go to your students' union or an outside organisation. They will listen to you sympathetically and take your complaint seriously. The increased media coverage of sexual assaults has meant that awareness of this issue is much greater and the way victims are supported has improved in recent years.

If you do go to an outside organisation rather than your students' union, you should still let the union know if the aggressor is associated with the university as they will want to take disciplinary action. It is a hard thing to do but, if you don't report the attack, that person will remain free to assault again. For ways of protecting yourself against attack see Safety and Security, chapter 8.

## Drugs

University is the first time many people come across drugs. You should be aware of the addictive properties, health risks and effects of any drug if you are tempted to experiment. It may be difficult, but do not feel pressurised into taking anything you have even the slightest doubt about. It is far better to cope with a small amount of teasing than the potentially devastating effects of drug misuse. You can develop a dependency on some illegal drugs very quickly and this can have serious repercussions on your health and life. It is not worth experimenting for the sake of being one of the crowd.

I found this idea that students sit around all the time smoking dope was completely unfounded. People on my corridor never smoked. I had to open all the windows and stuff a towel under the door if I wanted the occasional joint because of the disapproval of my fellow students.

*Third-year student, Loughborough University*

Injecting illegal drugs is a very dangerous business. The drug may have been mixed with another substance, which could be lethal, and the risk of accidental overdose and addiction is greater. There is also a very high risk of infection in the injection area as germs present on the skin are forced directly into the bloodstream. Inexpert and frequent injection can even cause the veins to collapse.

The reason why Edinburgh is the AIDS
capital of the UK is because there is no
needle exchange programme. Our students
are aware of the situation and don't really get
involved in the hard drugs scene.

*President of the Students' Association, Edinburgh University*

You are unlikely to come across most of the drugs mentioned in this section. They are all described here so that you
know the risks – both to your life and your liberty. Don't
believe anybody who tells you these dangers don't exist.

### Class A drugs
These are the drugs that carry the highest maximum
prison sentences: seven years and a fine for possession,
and life plus a fine for trafficking.

A real danger with any of these drugs that affect your
mind is that, if you are feeling uncertain or paranoid
about any aspect of life, your feelings will be exaggerated.
The power of bad trips should never be underestimated:
they can be relived a long time afterwards.

Ecstasy or MDMA is usually produced in the form of a
white, yellow, pink or brown tablet. It gives users a surge
of energy and the effects can last for several hours.
However, it can also lead to feelings of extreme paranoia
and insomnia. Recent studies have suggested that ecstasy
use may lead to permanent brain damage.

As with all stimulants it is more dangerous for people
with high blood pressure, epilepsy or heart conditions to
take it. It is also impossible to tell what is in an ecstasy
tablet: you could be taking ecstasy mixed with anything
from heroin to cleaning powders.

The hallucinogenic drugs that are most commonly
seen are magic mushrooms and LSD (acid). Magic mushrooms grow wild in many parts of the country and,

although it is not illegal to pick them and eat them raw, drying them out could result in a criminal charge. LSD is manufactured illegally in minute quantities which are impregnated into small pieces of blotting paper. The effect of hallucinogens varies according to the surroundings and whether the person feels happy and comfortable or not. Users may also experience 'flashback' where the trip is relived afterwards. Inexperienced users may feel disoriented and confused. If you are worried about someone in this state then stay with them and if the feelings do not pass call a doctor.

Cocaine and crack are very expensive and the effects are short-lived. Users can become addicted quite quickly; however, this does not mean that if you know someone who has taken one of these drugs they are, or will automatically become, an addict. The same is true of heroin. It can take weeks or months of heavy heroin misuse before someone becomes physically addicted.

### Class B drugs

Class B drugs carry maximum penalties of five years imprisonment for possession and 14 years for trafficking. You can be fined for each offence.

Cannabis, also known as dope, grass or hash, is the most commonly used drug on the student scene. It gives users a heightened sense of colour and sound. Like alcohol, it impairs co-ordination so you should not drive or operate machinery and should also be extra careful when crossing roads. It has no specific addictive properties but people can become psychologically dependent on the drug for relaxation or enjoyment.

Amphetamine, commonly known as 'speed', is the most commonly used illegal stimulant. It gives people a heightened sense of energy but can have some nasty side effects such as insomnia, loss of appetite and uncomfortable itching which can lead to anxiety or paranoia. Some people feel unwell for a long time when they stop taking speed after continuous use.

## Class C drugs

These drugs carry maximum prison sentences of two years and a fine for possession, and five years and a fine for trafficking.

Class C drugs include tranquillisers and mild amphetamines which doctors can prescribe to patients. Some people develop a psychological dependence on these drugs very quickly and find it difficult to come off them. If you are in this position then you should seek professional help. If your doctor prescribes these drugs to you and you are unhappy about taking them, remember that you have the right to seek a second opinion.

## Tobacco and alcohol

Tobacco and alcohol are legal drugs providing the age restrictions are obeyed. They are also the most socially acceptable drugs but can be highly addictive. The dangers associated with tobacco and regularly drinking too much alcohol have been widely documented.

There is this guy at college who is extremely intelligent. He has developed a very serious drinking problem, partly exacerbated by family tragedy. It is very difficult to know what to do when you see someone regularly hitting the bottle at 10 am.

*Second-year student, University of London*

The current recommended MAXIMUM weekly allowance of alcohol is 21 units for men and 14 units for women. This equates to 10 pints of normal strength beer or lager for men and seven pints for women. Alternatively, if you drink spirits, men should not drink more than 21 single measures and women more than 14. Regularly drinking in excess of this means you are putting a great deal of strain on your liver, brain, heart and nervous system.

My friends and I sat down the other week and worked out how much we drank. It was quite frightening; we all regularly drank over the weekly limit. The problem is that most students can be found in the bar of an evening and you tend to measure yourself against your peers so don't realise there is anything unusual about your habits.

*Third-year student, University of London*

Because alcohol is so much a part of the social scene in all walks of life it is often very difficult to refuse when somebody offers to buy you a drink. This is especially true in the first few weeks of university when you are desperately trying to fit in and don't want to appear 'square'. However, a slight loss of face is preferable to forcing yourself to do something you do not want to do.

I see a lot of students who develop a dependency on alcohol. It starts when they start drinking regularly for the first time when they arrive at university and then, as the pressures of college build up, they turn to it to relieve these pressures. It never works. They end up with far more problems than they started with. A missed essay or homesickness can never be solved if someone has an alcohol problem as well.

*Welfare Officer, Aberystwyth University*

## The emotional impact of student life

There are two key pieces of advice welfare officers round the country give to new students coping with living and learning away from home. The first is not to be embarrassed about admitting to any problems you might have; welfare advisers and sabbatical officers have encountered them all before. Secondly, you should not feel inferior if it seems that everyone else is handling the transition well; they are probably thinking exactly the same thing about you.

So, if you do experience difficulties remember that there is a whole network of support and that people will deal with your problems in the strictest confidence. Don't just sit and suffer in silence.

My first thought when I got to university was "help, I want to go home". I arrived with two bags and had no idea of what had happened to my trunk, which was being shipped over from Northern Ireland. I transported my few belongings into my room, sat down, decided I didn't have anything to do – I certainly didn't have any unpacking – so decided to go and say hello to anyone I might bump into. Luckily everybody else had had the same idea.

*Fourth-year student, Edinburgh University*

Everybody's experience of leaving home and starting university is different but most people will have a few problems adjusting. Anyone who claims never to have had a second thought about the whole process is probably lying. The important thing to remember is that you are not alone.

You can try to avoid as many problems as possible by preparing well beforehand (see chapter 3). If you ensure that you have got your grant application in on time, you have spent time thinking about what you need to take and you have double-checked that your accommodation is habitable and available, then you are likely to have a much smoother transition.

## Student life doesn't suit everyone

However well you have prepared for your move to university, there are always a few people each year who feel they have done the wrong thing by coming to university. You are not a failure if you feel like this. The most important thing to do is to talk to one of the people mentioned above. They will be able to help to identify the cause of the problem and offer advice. Don't make any hasty decisions. Give yourself time to acclimatise to your new environment. If, after talking to people and considering their suggestions, you decide that you still want to leave, then make sure you are aware of the financial implications (see chapter 5, page 151).

I realised at the end of my first year that I had chosen the wrong course and college. I stayed on basically because it all seemed too daunting to make such a huge move and I had developed interests outside college. I am glad that I got my degree but feel as though I failed to make the most of university by not doing a course I was interested in. Mind you – the grass is always greener.

*Graduate, University of London*

## Dealing with loneliness

There is an old student adage which says that you spend your second two terms trying to lose the friends you made in the first few weeks. This is bound to be true of some people because you are surrounded by so many strangers, so don't worry if you feel you have nothing in common with the first people you meet.

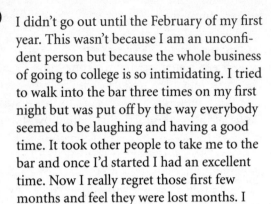

I didn't go out until the February of my first year. This wasn't because I am an unconfident person but because the whole business of going to college is so intimidating. I tried to walk into the bar three times on my first night but was put off by the way everybody seemed to be laughing and having a good time. It took other people to take me to the bar and once I'd started I had an excellent time. Now I really regret those first few months and feel they were lost months. I wish I had made the effort earlier.

*Undergraduate, now Welfare Officer, Lampeter University*

It is very easy, especially in the first few days, to look round the bar and believe that everyone has known each other for years. This is obviously not the case. All the first years are in exactly the same boat and those people who appear to be completely at ease are probably thinking that you look pretty cool too.

The thing is that we have been there before too, and recently enough to remember what it was like. I may be a welfare officer now but I still vividly remember being scared stupid when I first walked into the student bar. It is sometimes difficult for new students to appreciate this when they see that I am known by everyone in college.

*Welfare Officer, Lampeter University*

Don't worry if you don't get any further than the typical 'freshers' questions in the first few weeks. What's your name? Where do you come from? What A-levels did you do? What course are you on? Talk to any student and they will recognise those questions. They are what all first-year students have in common and are as good a starting point as any other. Use them if you are unsure about how to strike up a conversation.

> There are friends for everybody at university, it's just a case of finding a group you fit into. There will be one because of the diversity of people who go to college.

*Third-year student, Oxford University*

If you do find it difficult to make friends there are certain steps you can take to make things easier. You should not run home every weekend, but give yourself a chance to mix with your college peers. It is also important that you talk to someone about your difficulties. Your students' union will be extremely sympathetic to this problem as it is one which they encounter every year.

You should also not lose touch with the friends you have at home. Make special efforts to contact them during the holidays and invite them to come and stay with you at university. You may find it easier to join in college events if you have someone with you.

> A lot of the problems associated with homesickness in the first few weeks stem from a glossy picture of university and the expectations placed on new students. Don't expect to have a really wild time the whole time. Very few people have the money, or the stamina, to do this.

*Welfare Officer, Brighton University*

There are certain myths that surround student social life. The media tend to depict students as party animals who always have a choice of wild and exciting social engagements where they will get very drunk and sit around smoking joints. In reality this is not the case. Don't worry if there isn't a constant round of late night parties, club visits or outings to the cinema and theatre. After freshers' week you are much more likely to settle into a routine of pub visits and coffee-drinking sessions in various people's rooms. It isn't possible to have a wild and varied social calendar on a student grant, at least not if you want to eat as well.

When I first got to college I felt very unsure and lonely. I was daunted by the pressures of work, the whole business about being at Oxford and the idea that you should be able to do everything and do it well. I had no idea of what the parameters were and what I was allowed to get wrong. This had seemed quite obvious at school where I had felt very comfortable asking to be shown how to approach a question. I later found out that this was something I could do at university as well and realised that work was not the be all and end all of university life.

This just left the problem of how to make friends in this new environment. The best way I found of doing this was by joining the badminton and chess clubs. I made my closest friends at college, whom I know are going to be life-long friends, and with whom I have spent some of the best times ever.

*Graduate, Oxford University*

Finally, there are people who just like to be alone and there is absolutely nothing wrong with this. Solitude is only a problem if it makes you unhappy.

# Student welfare services

Increasingly the welfare of students in terms of facilities at the college (for example accommodation, academic problems and physical welfare) has passed out of the hands of universities. If you go to one of the Oxford or Cambridge colleges then you will have a personal tutor who is responsible for your educational and personal welfare, but in most other universities this role will be filled largely by your students' union or professional counsellors. Emotional or mental problems should be dealt with by a professional.

### Students' unions

Students' unions are impartial and can act as mediators between you and your department or outside organisations. The specific provisions and facilities students' unions can provide vary from university to university. Some will have well-equipped welfare centres with professional, sometimes specialist, counsellors for problems such as debt, while others will have a sabbatical officer responsible for welfare. Therapists and psychologists can be found in the health centre.

Whatever kind of welfare support is available in your university, students' unions have direct, often personal, experience of the problems facing their students. Sabbatical officers will have recent experience of being a student at your particular university and will be able to combine this with the professional training they have received in dealing with welfare matters. They can advise you on any problem you might encounter from financial, accommodation and educational difficulties to sexual, emotional and health worries.

Professional counsellors employed by students' unions are also chosen because of their experience in dealing with student problems.

If you smile and say hello to someone and they smile and say hello back then you have made a friend. Even if it is a friend to whom you just smile and say hello. Some people will do more than smile and say hello and you will have made a friend to go to the bar with or for a coffee.

*Welfare Officer, Loughborough University*

Many students' unions also run student nightline services. These are telephone help lines run and staffed entirely by students during the evening. They are great at sorting things out, from how to get home if you are stranded in the middle of nowhere to what you should do because nobody spoke to you tonight. The telephone numbers will be posted round the college or you can contact the head office (see the Lifesavers section, page 191) for the number of your nearest branch.

### The university
If the university provides welfare support for its students, the department will be called something like 'Student Services' although, again, this varies in different institutions. These departments are staffed by professional counsellors. They will work closely with the students' union's welfare sabbatical officer and so will be well aware of the problems facing students.

I found my tutor extremely sympathetic to the problems I had when I first came to university. There is no need to be embarrassed about talking about your difficulties. In fact, I had established such a rapport with her by the end of the first year that, when she had a dispute with the head of department, I was the one she turned to to talk things over.

*Second-year student, University of London*

You can go to your personal tutor with any problems you have; not just worries about your course. The disadvantage of relying on personal tutors is that you will have to make an appointment and lecturers are usually very busy people. However, they are the best people to advise you on study problems and, in some universities, this system of support is well established and is very successful.

## Outside organisations

If you do not feel like talking to someone associated with your university then you should contact one of the many local organisations with a speciality in the area in which you need help. You will have a wide choice, from debt counselling agencies and housing agencies to discrimination councils and legal aid centres. If you need advice in several areas, then your local Citizens' Advice Bureau is always a good point of contact. They have trained experts in every field imaginable and a huge referral and information system. Unfortunately, some Bureaux have had to cut down on the number of hours they open because of a lack of funding. You should always check when they are open and try to make an appointment.

You should always bring a stack of phone cards and your address book with you from home. Don't be afraid to let your friends and family know if you are having difficulties. It's remarkable what a chat with a familiar voice can do for your morale.

*Welfare Officer, Brighton University*

If you are seeking outside advice then a general tip is to go to independent organisations for help rather than the official, government departments. Independent organisations are often much better at looking at your particular needs and suggesting solutions. Government departments have to be concerned with making sure all the rules are followed and don't really have the time to sit down and work out what is best for your particular case.

## Lifesavers ⊗

### Organisations

Your students' union or university welfare department should probably be the first point of contact as they have experience of dealing with specific student-related problems.

Specialist outside organisations will be listed in the local phone book.

Acceptance Helpline and Support Group for Parents of Lesbians and Gay Men, 64 Holmside Avenue, Halfway Houses, Sheerness, Kent ME12 3EY, tel 0795 661463. Runs a national telephone helpline Tue–Fri 7–9pm, although you can try during the day as there are sometimes people around who can help. Disseminates information and holds meetings for parents.

Action on Smoking and Health (ASH), 109 Gloucester Place, London W1H 3PH. Will provide you with an information pack on how to give up smoking in return for a self-addressed envelope with a 36p stamp.

AIDS Care Education and Training, PO Box 1323, London W5 5TF, tel 081-840 7879. Has a volunteer work force of over 300 with a 24-hour team of doctors.

Al-Anon Family Groups, UK and Eire 61 Great Dover Street, London SE1 4YF, tel 071-403 0888. For friends and relatives of alcoholics.

Alcohol Concern, 375 Gray's Inn Road, London WC1X 8QF, tel 071-833 3471. A referral agency for people with alcohol problems. Callers are put in touch with a relevant local group. Also publishes leaflets and a fortnightly journal and has a library and information department.

Alcohol Concern Wales, Brunel House, Fitzalan Place, Cardiff CF2 3BA, tel 0222 488000

Alcoholics Anonymous – branches across the country. See your local phone book.

Anorexia Anonymous 081-748 3994 – a confidential advice agency for anorexics and bulimics which will offer free advice and therapy if required. Helpline open 8 am–9 pm Mon–Fri.

Anorexia and Bulimia Nervosa Association Helpline 081-885 3936. Tottenham Women's Centre, Tottenham Town Hall, Town Hall Approach, London N15 4RX. A confidential helpline open Wed 6–8.30 pm for women with eating disorders. There is also a drop-in centre open Wed 6.30–8 pm.

Body Positive, 51b Philbeach Gardens, London SW5 9EB, tel 071-835 1045. Helpline 071-373 9124 staffed by people who are HIV positive between 7–10 pm. They also run a youth and a women's support group. Ring the office for more details.

British Homeopathic Association, 7a Devonshire Road, London W1N 1RJ, tel 071-935 2163. Has a specialist lending library and a list of practising doctors, pharmacists and vets.

British Hypnotherapy Centre, 1 Wythburn Place, London W1H 5WL, tel 071-723 4443. If you write to them and indicate your problem, including the area where you live, they will send you a pamphlet of information and leaflets with the local registered practitioners in return for £2.

Brook Advisory Centres, 153a East Street, London SE17 2SD, tel 071-708 1390. Has centres across the country offering contraception, pregnancy tests and counselling on emotional and sexual problems for the under 25s. Publications are also available.

Drugline, 9a Brockley Cross, Brockley, London SE4 2AB, tel 081-692 4975. Telephone and individual advice and counselling.

Eating Disorders Association, Sackville Place, 44 Magdalen Street, Norwich NR3 1JE, tel 0603 621414. Youthline, tel 0603 765050.

Gamblers Anonymous and Gam-Anon, PO Box 88, London SW10 0EU, tel 071-384 3040. A self-help group for gamblers plus friendship and comfort for gamblers' families.

Lesbian and Gay Switchboard, tel 071-384 7324.

London Rape Crisis Centre – Helpline, tel 071-837 1600. Open Mon–Fri 10 am–11 pm, Sat & Sun 9 am–12 midnight. Offers counselling and help for women who have been victims of sexual violence (available to women outside London too).

National Association of Citizens Advice Bureaux (NACAB), 115–123 Pentonville Road, London N1 9LZ , tel 071-833 2181 There are over 1,000 CAB branches around the country. They can provide advice on many subjects including social security benefits, housing and financial and personal matters. They also have huge databases of information and can refer you to specialist independent organisations in the area.

Pregnancy Advice Service, 13 Charlotte Street, London W1P 1HD, tel 071-637 8962. A counselling and referral service, contraception advice and pregnancy testing.

Samaritans – Local Samaritans' numbers are in the front of phone books. They are extremely good at listening to all types of problems. You can talk to them 24 hours a day in complete confidence.

Standing Conference on Drug Abuse, 1–4 Hatton Place, Hatton Garden, London EC1N 8ND, tel 071-430 2341. Provides advice and information on available services; also a 24 hour freephone service on drugs problems giving recorded phone number contacts. You should phone the operator (100) and ask for freephone 'Drugs Services'.

Students' Nightline – National Co-ordinators, c/o Guild of Students, University of Birmingham, Edgbaston Park Road, Edgbaston, Birmingham B15 2TU. There are student nightline services operating in many universities across the country and they are growing in number. Complete confidentiality is guaranteed.

The Terrence Higgins Trust, 52–54 Gray's Inn Road, London WC1X 8JU, tel 071-831 0330. Helpline 071-242 1010 open 12 noon–10 pm. Legal line, tel 071-405 2381 open Wed 7–10 pm although you can try other times and/or ring the administration number. They are open seven days a week, all year and provide very friendly legal and welfare advice and counselling to people with AIDS and their friends and families. One-to-one sessions and self-help groups.

# 7 Travel

## Getting around at university

Travelling to and from college, and transport while you are there, can be an expensive business, especially if it is something you have not had to budget for before. If you can get a parent or a friend to drive you to university then do so. You won't lose any 'street cred' by having your parents arrive with you on your first day because most people will be in exactly the same position and it is well worth avoiding the possible embarrassment of an emotional public farewell at the railway station.

If you do have to travel to college on public transport then you will have to be particularly careful about what you take and how you pack it (see What to take with you, chapter 3). You may want to contact the bus, train or coach company you are travelling with to see if there are any special arrangements they can make for you to transport your belongings and store them during the journey. For instance, you can't take bikes on some train routes and there is often a luggage limit on coaches. You can arrange to have your belongings delivered to you by a courier company such as Red Star.

If you do have a lot of things to carry then plan your journey very carefully and allow plenty of time, particularly if it involves any changes. What is normally a leisurely five-minute stroll across a platform can be quite a different matter when you try to do this laden down like a pack mule, so avoid short connection times. You should also remember that you have to get from the station to the college. There is nothing more infuriating than carefully planning and negotiating a traumatic journey only to find you are stranded in a strange area and have no idea how you are going to get to the university. You should phone before you leave and get details about how to get there, including the cost of a taxi from the station, as this may well be a worthwhile investment.

It is also worth really interrogating the British Rail (BR) ticket office about the cheapest fare you can get. There will be days when it is cheaper to travel and there are also pre-booking schemes, such as Apex and Super Apex fares, which are very much cheaper. You will have to catch a certain train and give notice if you want to cancel your booking, but you should contact your local BR station at least a month before you need to travel to university and ask them about such schemes.

The methods of travel you have open to you will depend on where you are studying. If you study at a university in a small town then your feet or a bicycle are likely to be the best method of getting you from A to B, whereas if you study in London you will soon learn to do battle with the tube, bus and train networks.

I found that a car was actually cheaper to run and a hell of a lot more convenient than trying to rely on the non-existent public transport in Lampeter and Wales in general. Short of shelling out for taxis, there was no other way of effectively getting around on a regular basis.

*Third-year student, Lampeter University*

Many students find that a bike is a cheap and effective way of getting around, and most towns now include cycle tracks in their urban developments. The maintenance for a bicycle is much cheaper than for a motorbike or a car and it does help keep you fit. If you already have a car it probably isn't worth taking it to university. The tax, insurance (which may be more expensive for your university town than your home area), MOT, servicing and petrol will be a very big chunk of your not very large grant cheque and you may well find yourself inundated with requests for your chauffeur services. If you do find yourself ferrying friends on a regular basis you are allowed to accept payment to help cover your costs. But remember that you need a licence to taxi people for profit: if you don't have a licence you will find that your insurance is invalid. You won't have this problem if you own a motorbike but, unless you can maintain it cheaply yourself, the upkeep will probably be more expensive than using public transport.

If you do take your own transport to university, whether it is a bicycle, motorbike or car, you will need to have somewhere to keep it. You will also have to make sure that you can make adequate security arrangements. These are things to investigate before you travel to university.

When I moved out in my second year I
brought my bike back to college. A very
sensible move. It took me 15 minutes to cycle
into college whereas the local bus service only
ran every half hour and took much longer,
especially first thing in the morning.

*Second-year student, Oxford University*

Whatever form of transport you choose, it will be one of
the essentials you budget for (see Budgeting, chapter 1). If
you decide that public transport is the most useful to you,
and will have to travel regularly, you should find out
about getting travel cards. It may well work out cheaper
to buy a monthly or weekly travel card than to pay for
transport each day. Your students' union or the local station will be able to give you details.

If you have to travel regularly by train it is worth
buying a Young Person's Railcard. This will give you a
third off all your train journeys. It lasts for a year and all
full-time students can get one up to the age of 26. It is
available from all British Rail stations and you will need
to take proof of your student status with you.

### College schemes

Some students' unions run their own transport schemes.
These vary wildly and can range from a women's minibus
service late at night, to deals with local taxi firms for
students stranded with no means of getting home. Your
students' union will advertise such schemes during freshers' week so look out for the details.

Our minibus service is great. It runs every
half hour and the last one goes at 11.30 pm.
It runs from the university into town and
will take students into the outlying villages.

The only problem comes when one person wants a doorstep delivery to somewhere eight miles off course as this delays the whole service.

*Women's Officer, Swansea University*

## Travelling abroad

The years at university are often the only time when people have the freedom to explore far flung climes. However, it is also the time when this has to be done on a very strict budget. The travel operators have picked up on this and the competition is fierce for student discount flights. You should always shop around for the best quote.

The two largest student travel companies are Campus Travel and STA Travel, but look in the phone book as there may be local student travel companies in your area.

Whichever company you book through, always check to see if it is a member of the Association of British Travel Agents (ABTA), and if it isn't DON'T book a flight with it. ABTA acts as a guarantor for all agents registered with it so if the travel company fails to supply the goods your expenses should be refunded to you.

The cheapest way of flying will probably be by taking a courier flight. Look out for advertisements in the local and national press, as companies will pay a significant proportion of your flight in return for the use of your luggage space. This is probably not an option if you are travelling for a long period of time as you will have to fit all your belongings into your hand luggage. You may also be able to travel as a paid companion for young children or elderly people. All information about courier flights can be found in *The Courier Air Travel Handbook* by Mark Field, which is published by Spectrum. You will have your arrival and departure times set by the company which is using you as a courier.

I found that being able to speak another language was a big advantage when travelling. When I toured Eastern Europe I was able to use French and German to speak to people I met on trains. You should not shy away from making contact with people abroad as this is the best way to get to know about the country. You miss out on a whole dimension by not getting to know the local people. One woman I met in Prague showed us round the town and pointed out all the bullet holes, hidden unless you knew where to look.

*Fourth-year student, University of London*

Travelling by train might be a more viable option on your budget. You can get an Inter-rail card which will give you one month's unlimited second-class travel on European railways (excluding Albania and Russia). It costs £249 if you are under 26. If you are over 26, the card will cost £209 for 15 days or £269 for a month. You can buy it from any major British Rail station or through a student travel agent. If you are a non-European student and haven't been living in Europe for six months, then you won't qualify for an Inter-rail card, but you can get a Eurorail card, which allows you up to 15 days' travel within a two-month period.

The other discount card available is the Eurorail Pass. It costs £565 for any age. This gives you one month's unlimited travel but is only valid in a limited number of countries. The Eurorail Youth Pass is available to people under 26 and costs £395. You should check with a student travel operator for specific details.

Explorer tickets will allow you to travel along a pre-determined route for two months and stop off anywhere along the way. For example, the Eastern Europe Explorer would allow you to travel from Britain into Eastern Europe and includes the price of a ferry.

> You may have to develop a cast iron stomach when travelling. In Eastern Europe, where food was a luxury, they served meals in the station in shifts. There was one sitting at 1 pm and another at 2 pm. If you turned up for the later sitting then the food was just cold. I am not a fussy eater but I had to leave the grey soup which was bits of congealed fat floating around a bone with gristle hanging off it. I felt really guilty but it was the most disgusting thing I have ever tasted.

*Fourth-year student, University of London*

You should also look at travelling by coach. A coach ticket is certainly cheaper than a plane ticket but it will obviously take much longer. You will also have to pay for your food and accommodation en route. You can get tickets for the licensed Eurolines company from any National Express agent. There are unlicensed companies that will be cheaper but they might not follow all the safety laws that govern licensed companies.

> In Eastern Europe hitching was not particularly successful when we went because there was a general shortage of cars, and what cars were on the road were subject to petrol rationing so lots of people were car-sharing anyway.

*Second-year student, University of London*

If you think that hitching is the only way you can afford to travel then you should be mindful of the obvious security risks involved. Women should NEVER hitch alone. You should also find out about the laws which govern hitching abroad so you avoid hassles with the local police. Different countries have different hitching codes, so find out about the code that operates where you are. If you use the thumb signal in some countries you will actually be giving prospective lifts the equivalent of the V-sign, which isn't perhaps the best way to encourage people to pick you up. Vacation Work publishes *Europe: A Manual for Hitchhikers* by Simon Calder.

### Useful student cards

It is a good idea to get hold of an International Student Identity Card (ISIC), as this not only gives you discounts on student chartered flights but also on entry to museums, galleries, etc, abroad. You can get an ISIC card from a student travel operator for £5 providing you are following a course of higher education. Unfortunately for mature students, many of the discounts are restricted to students aged between 16 and 30.

> An ISIC card is a good idea. For instance the Prado museum in Madrid charges 500 pesetas admission normally, whereas if you have an ISIC card you can go in as often as you want for free.

*Third-year student, University of London*

You may also want to get hold of a Youth Hostel Association (YHA) card which will allow you to stay in youth hostels in 56 countries. They may not be the most luxurious places but they tend to be cheap and are good places to meet other people doing the same thing.

Students with an ISIC card can apply for an International Youth Hostel Federation (IYHF) card which will give them the same benefits and is available from the YHA head office (see Lifesavers). If you are planning to travel by moving from hostel to hostel then check out the entry requirements, such as whether they are single sex or not, before you leave.

## Accommodation abroad

Camping is a good, cheap form of accommodation while travelling. However, you should remember that some camp sites in towns are a fair distance from the centre, which might be a problem if local public transport isn't good. If you are travelling the countryside, though, this is not a problem and you can end up in some really beautiful areas.

Youth hostels vary quite considerably in the rules they enforce. They may be run by the Youth Hostelling Association or independently. Some youth hostels will have a certain time you have to be back and will expect you to do some chores. You may also be expected to sleep in single-sex dorms. Others are more lenient and allow men and women to share a single room, do not lock the doors at a certain time and allow you to cook your own meals. The independent hostels tend to be the ones that have fewer rules, but you should shop around to find the ones that best suit your needs.

We stayed in an excellent hostel in Dingle Bay where we shared a room with the two other guests. There was no separation of sexes and it was just like staying in a big house. The owners lived over the road and only came round to pick up the money.

*Second-year student, Edinburgh University*

Pensiones are cheap hotels, and you don't usually have to meet any particular criteria in order to stay there. You can stay in a single or shared room. The facilities vary though, and they often don't provide meals, so shop around. They can be very convenient, often situated in the centre of town.

You might find that hotels are a bargain abroad. This is particularly true in Eastern Europe, Asia and Africa where hotels are very cheap when judged by Western European standards.

Sleeping on beaches is obviously a free option but you should be careful that you are not robbed during the night. In some countries thieves are very adept and can take your rucksack out from under you while you are asleep.

If you are Inter-railing you can kill two birds with one stone and save money on accommodation by arranging to travel to your next destination on an overnight train. You have to be careful though if your destination is not the last one, and make sure you wake up in time. You should also watch out for your luggage – sleeping travellers are a common target for thieves.

I tried to travel overnight from Milan to Venice but when I woke up I had a horrible feeling I had overslept. I had to try and ask the Italian guard, with no Italian, where we were. It turned out I was nearly in Slovenia.

*Fourth-year student, University of London*

Sleeping in train stations is free, but is not a particularly comfortable option. You will find that some stations won't allow you to sleep there and have security guards who throw you out. You can tell the ones who don't mind you dossing down because there will be other people doing the same thing. You should sleep near other people for security reasons and, again, be careful about being robbed.

## Checklist for travelling abroad

❏ Make sure your passport is valid for the duration of your holiday!

❏ Check with the embassy to see if you need a visa.

❏ Make sure you have had all the necessary injections (ask your doctor).

❏ Take some basic medicines with you, including sun cream and mosquito repellent as these are not always easy to get.

❏ Take a toilet roll.

❏ Check the availability of contraception as you cannot always buy condoms over the counter.

❏ Invest in a good quality penknife.

❏ Take a travel alarm clock: it will be really useful if you have early trains to catch.

❏ If you are camping check your tent before you leave, it may be too late to get more tent pegs when you are there. You should also take a mallet and roll mats.

❏ You should take a sleeping bag even if you are not camping.

❏ In some countries it is better to have US dollars, so you may want to take traveller's cheques in dollars and some dollars in cash.

❏ Carry all money in a money belt UNDER your clothes.

❏ Invest in a *Rough Guide* or a *Lonely Planet Guide* for the country/countries you will be travelling in: they contain all the information you will need to find out in one place. Tourist Information offices can be difficult to find and are not always open.

❏ Invest in a good quality rucksack.

❏ Do not take too many clothes with you. Just make sure you have something waterproof, something warm and something cool, something to protect you from the sun, and that you have a very comfortable pair of boots or shoes.

❏ Do not pack your rucksack too full as you may want to collect things on the way.

❏ Do not take anything valuable with you. Leave your jewellery and Rolex watch at home.

# Lifesavers ⊗

## Airports

London: City Airport,
    tel 071-474 5555
Gatwick,
    tel 0293 535353
Heathrow,
    tel 081-759 4321

Stansted,
    tel 0279 680500
Luton,
    tel 0582 405100
Manchester International,
    tel 061-489 3000

## British Rail stations

British Rail International
    Centre, Victoria British
    Rail station, London
    SW1V 1JY,
    tel 071-834 2345
London: Charing Cross,
    tel 071-928 5100
Euston,
    tel 071-387 7070
Kings Cross,
    tel 071-278 2477
Liverpool Street,
    tel 071-928 5100
Paddington,
    tel 071-262 6767
St Pancras,
    tel 071- 387 7070

Victoria,
    tel 071-928 5100.
Waterloo,
    tel 071-928 5100
Birmingham New Street,
    tel 021-643 2711
Edinburgh Waverly,
    tel 031-556 2451
Glasgow Central Union
    Street, tel 041-204 2844
Liverpool Lime Street,
    tel 051-709 9696
Manchester Piccadilly,
    tel 061-832 8353

## Other addresses

British Universities North America Camp, 232 Vauxhall Bridge Road, London SW1V 1AU.

Campus Travel/Eurotrain, 52 Grosvenor Gardens, London SW1W OAG, tel 071-730 3402/8111.

Eurolines, 52 Crawley Road, Luton, Bedfordshire, LU1 1HX, tel 0582 404511.

Passport Office, Clive House, 70–80 Petty France, London SW1H 9HD, tel 071-834 4000/071-279 3434. You can get forms from the Post Office which give the address of your nearest passport office.

STA Travel Head Office, 6 Wrights Lane, London W8 6TA, tel 071-938 4711.

Victoria Coach Station, Buckingham Palace Road, London SW1, tel 071-730 0202.

YMCA Inter-rail Programme, Crown House, 550 Muldeth Road West, Chorlton, Manchester M21 2SJ, tel 061-881 5321.

Youth Hostelling Association (YHA) Trevelyn House, 8 St Steven's Hill, St Albans, Hertfordshire AL1 2DY, tel 0727 855215. Open 9 am–5.30 pm Mon–Fri.

## Publications

*Adventure Holidays,* Vacation Work at 9 Park End Street, Oxford OX1 1HJ. An annual publication which costs £5.95.

*Europe: A Hitchhiker's Manual,* Vacation Work, £3.95.

*Get up and Go – A Survival Kit for Women,* Attic Press, £6.99.

*International Youth Hostel Handbook,* volumes 1 and 2, YHA Services, £5.99 each. Write to YHA Services, 14 Southampton Street, London WC2E 7HY, tel 071-836 8541.

*Let's Go* guides, cover a wide variety of countries for around £14.99 each.

*Lonely Planet Guides,* give very good, comprehensive information on a wide range of countries: includes medical advice and some historical contexts.

*Rough Guides*, cover the same information as above on European countries at an affordable price (about £8.99) in an easy to follow style.

*The Courier Air Travel Handbook*, Spectrum, £6.99.

*Working Holidays*, Central Bureau for Educational Visits and Exchanges, Seymore Mews House, Seymore Mews, London W1H 9PE.

*Work Your Way Round The World*, Vacation Work. A biannual publication costing £9.95.

# 8 Safety and Security

Safety is still something that women have to be more concerned about than men. Many students' unions run women's self-defence classes and minibus services, and issue all new women students with a personal safety alarm when they first arrive at university. It is definitely worth taking up these options if your union provides them.

However, safety is something both men and women should be aware of, particularly when they first arrive, as there are greater risks in an area you do not know well. Men should also be conscious of the safety concerns of women so they can avoid making them feel threatened. The following 'dos' and 'don'ts' will highlight the dangers and show you how to avoid them.

## General safety

Some unions will take first-year students on trips into town and show them any areas to avoid. Even if your students' union doesn't have such a scheme it will be able to tell you if there are certain areas you should avoid. Generally you should stay well clear of poorly lit areas and avoid travelling around late at night by yourself, at least until you get to know the area better.

The most important thing you can do to protect your safety is avoid potentially dangerous situations and be alert to your surroundings.

☛ DON'T take short cuts through unlit or unpopulated areas.

☛ DON'T dawdle along in a world of your own.

☛ DON'T listen to your personal stereo.

☞   DON'T walk close to bushes and hedges.

☞   DON'T have a regular routine whereby you always walk back at the same time and follow the same route.

☞   DON'T carry a weapon, it may be used against you.

☞   DO stick to well-lit streets.

☞   DO be alert and look back occasionally to see if you are being followed.

☞   DO walk at a brisk pace and purposefully.

☞   DO carry a personal safety alarm and keep it somewhere accessible.

☞   DO, if walking through a dodgy area, wear unisex clothes or at least shoes you can run in.

☞   DO walk with a friend if possible. This is one of the advantages of living in an area well-populated by students.

If you are attacked then shout as loudly as you can. Don't scream, but shout 'NO': some male attackers get a kick out of hearing a woman scream. If you think you are being followed then go to the nearest lit house and ask to use the phone. Always run if you can and only fight back if you can't escape. Poking your fingers in your attacker's eyes is effective and unexpected. Stamping on someone's foot or kicking them in the shins will surprise them and may loosen their grip.

## At home

☞   DON'T hide your keys outside.

☞   DON'T enter if you notice there is something unusual, the intruder may still be inside.

☛   DO have your keys already in your hand. They can also act as a useful weapon.

☛   DO make sure there is adequate lighting which illuminates all potential hiding places.

If your house is broken into or the lock tampered with in any way then have the locks changed immediately. You should also contact your local police crime prevention desk as they will be more than happy to offer you free advice on how to improve the security of your home.

☛   DON'T leave doors and windows open – keep them locked.

☛   DON'T let strangers in to use the phone: they may be burglars checking for valuables.

☛   DON'T invite strangers in, even if they say they are a friend of one of your flatmates.

☛   DON'T tell people who ring that you are alone.

☛   DO draw all curtains and blinds.

☛   DO fit and use a door chain.

☛   DO keep lights on.

☛   DO lock your bedroom door if possible.

☛   DO ask to see identification of any 'officials' who call.

You should report all suspicious incidents to the police and make sure you can escape quickly if necessary. This means knowing where your keys are and making sure any emergency exits are kept in good repair.

## On the move

### Public transport

☛   DON'T wait at isolated and empty bus stops and stations.

☞   DON'T get into an empty compartment or one with just one other passenger in it if you have a choice.

☞   DON'T strike up conversations with strangers or accept any invitations to get off the public transport and walk you home.

☞   DO sit next to the driver, conductor or, if you are a woman, another woman.

☞   DO complain to a driver, conductor, guard or other person in authority if you are pestered or made to feel awkward.

☞   DO make sure you leave plenty of time to catch the last bus, train or tube, particularly if you have connections to make.

You should find out whether your students' union runs its own alternative transport. This will often be much cheaper, and definitely safer, than relying on public transport.

### Taxis

☞   DON'T take a ride in unmarked cars claiming to be taxis.

☞   DO ask mini-cab drivers for their identification or make a note of the black cab number.

☞   DO plan well in advance and use a reputable firm.

☞   DO ask for a woman driver if travelling alone late at night.

Some students' unions run schemes in conjunction with local taxi firms, whereby you can hand over your union card if you haven't got the money to get back home. The firm then invoices the union and you pay when you pick up your card.

# Tactical tips

## How men can help

- ☞ DON'T walk down the same side of the street as a lone woman at night: she might think you are following her.

- ☞ DON'T pass comment on or try to strike up a conversation with a woman travelling by herself. You may just want to be friendly and helpful but this is not the right time. A woman has to treat you as if you are a potential threat.

- ☞ DON'T get into a compartment at night if there are only one or two women sitting there already.

- ☞ DON'T follow a woman into an alleyway or unpopulated area at night.

- ☞ DO offer to see women friends home and arrange to meet women flatmates and travel back home with them at night.

- ☞ DO volunteer to participate in any campus escort schemes run by your union, where male students walk female students back to their halls of residence after union events.

## Violence against men

Men also get mugged and raped and, if you are a gay man, then you may experience violence in the form of 'gay-bashing'. The safety guidelines given apply equally to men as well as to women. It is really important that you do not see admitting to an attack as a reflection on your manhood. There is nothing to be ashamed of. The police, your students' union and the specialist outside organisations are all well aware that men experience violence, and are practised in dealing with assaults against men. Report the attack and seek help.

## Defending yourself

If your students' union runs a self-defence course then you might consider signing up for it. Self-defence courses teach you to protect yourself if you find yourself in a dangerous situation, and also how to avoid these situations in the first place. They teach you a whole attitude to life and will give you confidence because you know what to do if you are attacked.

> You can always tell when the self-defence courses are being run here because all the guys are covered in bruises where the women have been practising on us.

*Third-year student, Edinburgh University*

# Lifesavers ⊗

Whether you are male or female you must seek assistance if you are attacked. Report the crime to the police and get counselling. You will need professional help to come to terms with what has happened to you. The police will be able to put you in touch with local groups.

# 9 Students with Disabilities

The problem with a society that is structured round able-bodied people is that it is often responsible for further disabling a person who has an impairment. You should not be afraid to spell out your needs. Many university students still come from very sheltered backgrounds and have not met anybody who has a disability before, so you will have to be prepared to educate them.

> The best thing I can say is that no matter what your disability, be it as obvious as being in a wheelchair, or 'hidden' such as visual impairment or dyslexia, once you have begun your course (and even before) you should keep in regular contact with your teaching staff to let them know what sorts of things they should do to enable you to follow your course. You may also find it helpful to contact a specialist organisation to advise your lecturers on what they can do.
>
> I know from my own experience that, if you don't tell people, be they lecturers or fellow students, they are not going to know how to help you. I know this is not easy and that it is not something we, as disabled students, should have to do. However, we do not live in a perfect society and, hard as this is, and much as we feel we should be given support and assistance as a right, if we don't make others in the university aware of our individual needs, then things will never improve.

*Second-year student, Nottingham Trent University*

# Choosing a university

I used my interview as an opportunity to "sound out" what I thought the attitudes and thoughts of some of the staff would be towards having a student with a disability on their course. Although it has to be said that hardly any of the lecturers I spoke to then had any idea of what sort of special arrangements would have to be made, I nevertheless felt there was a genuine willingness to listen and at least to try to understand.

*Second-year student, Nottingham Trent University*

It is vitally important that you go and see a university before you study there. You should contact the university before you fill in your UCAS form and check to see it can help with any special facilities you need. Most colleges have someone who is responsible for students with special needs and the sooner you tell them about your situation the longer it gives them to arrange the support you require.

I am a wheelchair user and was told that there were facilities for wheelchair access, which is true. What I was not told is that Aberystwyth is on a pretty enormous hill and the campus is on many different levels and therefore, although some of the buildings do have wheelchair access, actually getting to them is not practicable.

*First-year student, Aberystwyth University*

Universities and students' unions often publish leaflets which provide information on disabled access and special needs provisions in their institutions. SKILL, which is the National Bureau for Students with Disabilities, also produces a series of guides to higher education which give more general information on what is available in the universities around the country. If you are refused a place at a university because of your disability then UCAS will allow you to make another choice. Contact UCAS for details (see General Directory page 234).

### Living away from home

Learning to live away from the parental home is difficult for any student. If you have special needs then you should let the accommodation office know as soon as possible and ask for any modifications you need. It may be a good idea to live in college accommodation as this will enable you to become fully integrated into university life and may lessen any mobility difficulties you have. The accommodation provision for students with special needs varies around the country. Some institutions are very good and some are very bad, but the more vocal you are the more universities will realise how short they fall.

It should be the university's responsibility not to disable you by providing facilities which you cannot use. However, you can't judge the facilities properly until you see them for yourself, so make sure you arrange to visit the university. Some universities organise special needs days separately from interview days where you can go round and talk to the department, the union and the accommodation office about what they can do to help you.

In my case I had to explain to the other people who lived in my hall of residence that, although I am severely partially sighted, this does not mean I cannot see anything. This also doesn't mean that there aren't times when a little friendly support and

encouragement wouldn't come amiss, such
as a friendly shoulder to grab hold of when
we go to the bar.

*Second-year student, Nottingham Trent University*

Specialist equipment and help can be arranged in conjunction with the social services in your university town.
You should contact them as soon as you accept a place so
they have plenty of time to work with the university. They
may not be able to help because of budgetary restrictions
but it's worth asking.

### Travel

You may have particular difficulties travelling backwards
and forwards from university, so plan well in advance and
sort out transport for you and your belongings at the
beginning and end of term.

If you need help on a daily basis then speak to the university about any schemes it has. You should also ask it
about local transport schemes run for people with disabilities. The local council will be able to give you specific
details.

You can't expect your lecturers automatically
to realise that because you are in a wheelchair it will take you longer to get from place
to place unless you tell them.

*First-year student, Aberystwyth University*

### Studying

Again, the support service for special needs students
varies from university to university and can range from
induction loops in all lecture theatres to dyslexic support
groups. The facilities offered will influence where you
choose to study so contact the college for details before
you put in your UCAS form. Once a university has given

you a place it will be very willing to make any arrangements you need to enable you to study efficiently.

> Although I was aware of what special arrangements had been made for me to take my A-levels, most of the real issues I would have to tackle only became clear once I had had a chance to see how different a degree course is to an A-level one. Disabled or not, university staff have a completely different attitude to sixth-form staff. They aren't there to watch over you, make sure you attend every lecture and hound you for essays. The emphasis is much more on you. For a disabled student, if you do not speak to lecturers personally and make them aware of your specific needs, then things can become very difficult.

*Second-year student, Nottingham Trent University*

The NUS publishes a pack, *Students with Disabilities*, which provides information to universities and students' unions showing how special needs can be met, and which can be used as a general guide. There is also an information sheet produced by SKILL, *Identifying the Needs of Students with Disabilities in Further and Higher Education*, which is free and very useful in determining what support universities can provide.

You will also be able to make special arrangements to take your exams. Departments will be more than happy to accommodate you but you should talk to them well in advance.

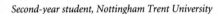

## Money matters

You will be entitled to a mandatory grant for your course providing you fulfil the criteria laid out in chapter 1. As a student with disabilities you will also be able to claim additional allowances from your grant allocation authority. These fall under the general heading of Disabled Students' Allowance and are divided into three categories. They are intended to meet the extra costs you incur because of your disability. They are all means-tested so will depend on the generosity of your LEA and on how well you are able to support your claim.

All LEAs have their own policies for assessing whether you qualify, so you should ask yours for details when you apply for your grant. It may ask you to support your claim with a letter from your doctor or the university, or with assessment details from a recognised relevant organisation.

### 1    General allowance

This is intended to meet any additional study costs you have because of your disability. For instance, you may require typing or transcription services.

### 2    Specialist equipment allowance

This is a one-off payment and can be used, for example, to buy computer equipment, Braille equipment or induction loops.

### 3    Non-medical personal helper allowance

This is money which can be used to help you fully participate in university life. You could use it to pay for a sign-language interpreter, someone to take your notes or to help you travel around the university.

### Travel costs

You can also claim for help with any additional travel costs you have. This is measured against what it would cost for an able-bodied student to make the same journey. You should keep accurate records of all your travel expenses as you will usually have to submit your claim to the LEA at the end of term.

### Benefits

As a student with disabilities you may be able to claim income support, housing benefit and other benefits, such as the mobility allowance and the attendance allowance, to cover additional costs you incur because of your disability. You have to meet certain criteria to qualify for these benefits so contact SKILL, your local social security office or a local independent advice organisation such as the Citizens' Advice Bureau before you fill out any claim forms.

### Student loans

You are entitled to apply for a student loan in the same way as any other student. You may be able to make special arrangements to pay back the loan if you are worried that your disability will affect your earning prospects after you graduate. Speak to the special needs officer at your university for advice on how to arrange this with the Student Loans Company.

### Access funds

The rules which govern access funds are set by the individual universities (see chapter 1 for details) and there is no general provision that students with disabilities should be given priority. Speak to your students' union about the criteria which operate at your university.

### What happens if there is not enough money?

Most students have debts during their time at university and have to rely on bank overdrafts, but students with disabilities may find particular difficulties meeting their expenses. If you find yourself in this position then you should contact SKILL for a list of charities, trusts and local groups which may be able to help you.

## Social life

This may not seem like the most important thing to sort out when you are facing the mountain of organisation involved in moving to university, but of course you do want to get the most out of college life. When you are applying, talk to students' unions about access and the provisions they can make to enable you to participate. Most students' unions have done a lot of work in recent years to make things easier, although provisions do vary. You may find there are specific support groups for students with your needs and, if not, you could think about setting one up (see Getting involved in university life, chapter 4). Some of the responsibility for making other students aware of students with disabilities will inevitably fall on your shoulders.

As a student with a disability it may not be as easy to participate in university life as it is for your able-bodied friends: it may require more determination and you may not be able to do everything, but why let this stop you? I found I needed to hang on to someone's shoulder very tightly in dark and dingy night clubs. It probably did look a bit peculiar, a six foot three man hanging onto a five foot eight man's shoulder for no apparent reason but, after a while, my friends just accepted it as something which had to be done.

*Second-year student, Nottingham Trent University*

You should also find out as much as you can about local groups and facilities. It will be pretty miserable if there are no pubs, cinemas or clubs in town which have disabled access. However, some areas have very active local groups and you can find out about these by contacting the local library or Citizens' Advice Bureau. You can also try looking in the local phone book for specialist organisations.

Sporting students should contact the union officer with responsibility for running the sports clubs. The

British Sports Association for the Disabled will be able to give you or your union specific advice.

## Sex and sexuality

Media stereotypes tend to portray people with disabilities as non-sexual. This is, of course, not true. You have as much sexual desire as any other student, and university will often be the place where you have the time and freedom to express it. You may have to be more open with your partner and talk through your emotional and physical needs. However, this will often provide a very strong basis for a relationship and you should look at it as a positive aspect of your sexuality. SPOD, the association to aid the sexual and personal relationships of people with a disability, will be able to give you and your partner any specific advice you need. You can also talk to your students' union welfare counsellor in complete confidence, or perhaps one of the specialist organisations if you prefer to speak to someone who has similar experiences to your own.

# Lifesavers ⊗

## Organisations

You may want to contact the specialist organisation concerned with your disability. It will have come across other students in your position and may be able to offer a few pointers.

British Dyslexia Association, 98 London Road, Reading, Berkshire RG1 5AU, tel 0734 662677 (administration). Helpline, tel 0734 668271 open 10 am–12.45 pm and 2–5 pm Mon–Fri.

British Sports Association for the Disabled, The Mary Glenhaig Suite, Solecast House, 13–27 Brunswick Place, London N1 6DX, tel 071-490 4919.

DGCIS (Disabled Graduate Careers Information Service), The University of Reading, Bulsmere Court,

Woodlands Avenue, Earley, Reading RG6 1HY, tel 0734 318659.

DIAL UK (National Association of Disablement Information and Advice Lines), Park Lodge, St Catherine's Hospital, Tickhill Road, Balby, Doncaster, South Yorkshire DN4 8QN, tel 0302 310123. They can put you in touch with local groups.

DIG (Disablement Income Group), Unit 5, Archway Business Centre, 19–23 Wedmore Street, London N19 4RZ, tel 071-263 3981.

Disability Alliance, Universal House, 88–94 Wentworth Street, London E1 7SA, tel 071-247 8776. Advice line on benefit problems, tel 071-247 8763, open 11 am–3 pm Mon–Fri. Also publishes disability rights handbooks at £7.95 including postage (£5 for benefit receivers).

Dyslexia Institute, 133 Gresham Road, Staines TW18 2AJ, tel 0784 463935.

Electronic Aids Loans for Disabled People, Willow Brook, Swanbourne Road, Buckingham MK17 0JA.

MIND (National Association for Mental Health), 22 Harley Street, London W1N 2ED, tel 071-637 0741. Open 9.15 am–5.15 pm Mon–Fri.

National Union of Students with Disabilities Campaign, 461 Holloway Road, London N7 6LJ, tel 071-272 8900.

RADAR (Royal Association for Disability and Rehabilitation), 25 Mortimer Street, London W1N 8AB, tel 071-637 5400.

Royal National Institute for the Blind (RNIB), 224 Great Portland Street, London W1N 6AA, tel 071-388 1266. Runs a student support service and benefits rights office.

Royal National Institute for the Deaf (RNID), 105 Gower Street, London WC1E 6AH, tel 071-387 8033. Runs a higher education communication support service with information on how you can get the support you need.

SKILL: National Bureau for Students with Disabilities, 366 Brixton Road, London SW9 7AA, tel 071-274 0565. Runs an information and advice service on all aspects of post-16 education for young people and adults with disabilities and learning difficulties. Publishes comprehensive guides and information sheets on all aspects of post-16 education. Contact them for full details.

SPOD (Association to aid the sexual and personal relationships of people with a disability), 286 Camden Road, London N7 0BJ, tel 071-607 8851/2.

TRIPSCOPE, 63 Esmond Road, London W4 1JE, tel 081-994 9294. Provides information and advice on transport systems at home and abroad for people with disabilities. Open 9.30 am–5 pm Mon–Fri.

# 10  Discrimination

Discrimination is an unfortunate fact of life and comes in many forms. If you feel you have been treated in a prejudiced way then you have been discriminated against. You don't have to be black, a woman, homosexual, come from a different country or have different cultural roots to experience discrimination, although bigoted individuals do tend to focus on these particular groups.

Many universities and students' unions have been taking very overt steps to try to eradicate discrimination as far as possible in the higher education sector. It is now common to find an equal opportunities policy in universities. However, discrimination still exists in universities as it does in the world outside.

The following forms of discrimination are the ones that most frequently occur, which is why they have been selected. This is not an exhaustive list and you should speak to the college authorities or your students' union, whatever form of discrimination you suffer.

Modern British fascists believe that this country should only be populated by white people born and bred in England. They will also target gay and overseas students.

The particularly nasty thing about fascists is that they express their prejudices in a violent way. What you should remember if you are being harassed by a fascist is that they are definitely in the minority and their behaviour will not be tolerated by the vast majority of students.

We had some big problems here because the British Nationalist Party (BNP) has a strong base in the local community. We discovered that one of our students had been asked to

recruit members from among the new
freshers. The students' union took him to a
full disciplinary hearing with the university
and he was banned from college for a year.

*Union President, University of London*

Fascists can be very intimidating but you should speak up at once, even if they have threatened you, as there are things that can be done to stop them. Your students' union can ban students with fascist prejudices from the union and, if their behaviour is violent, take them before a formal hearing with the university. Your students' union can also give you advice on how to protect yourself if you have been threatened with violence.

I once got a letter from the BNP criticising
the newspaper for not giving them enough
coverage and writing a story in a biased way.
Goodness knows what coverage they
expected after they had shouted verbal abuse
and incited violence against an anti-fascism
march. Why they thought their deeply
prejudiced views would get exposure in a
student newspaper, I really can't work out,
especially as the week before we had run an
interview with some French students in
which they described their horrific
experiences of fascism because they had
spoken out against Le Pen's regime.

*Sabbatical Editor, University of London*

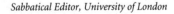

## Racial minorities

The ethnic mix at your university will depend on where you go to study. Some universities have a very wide cultural range of students and others are still white enclaves.

Wherever you go, you may be the first black or Asian person some white students have encountered on a day-to-day basis and you may have to let them know if they are – however unknowingly – behaving in a prejudiced way. White students should be aware of the potential for racism and make an effort to put a stop to it.

> I found that I experienced less racism in college than I did outside. It is frightening the number of people who will pass comment on you as you are walking down the street just because you happen to be black. I found my fellow students were more open-minded and more accepting. The problem comes when black students go out into the world expecting it to be as friendly as university.

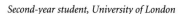

*Second-year student, University of London*

The Committee of Vice-Chancellors and Principals has a free publication called *Racial Harassment: Guidance for Universities* in which it defines racial harassment as 'the behaviour that creates an intimidating, hostile or offensive environment for study and social life'. If you feel you have been subjected to this then there are several places you can turn to. Your students' union may have several relevant societies, it may also have a black officer, and will certainly have a welfare officer. They will be able to offer you advice on how to pursue a complaint. If the level of racism you have suffered is severe you may want to get advice from the Commission for Racial Equality and take your complaint to the police. The National Union of Students has an Anti-Racism Committee which organises campaigns against racism in universities and the community in general and will be happy to help you.

> I went out with a girl who was black. I found our friends in college were very supportive of the relationship, although I did sometimes wonder whether that was because of her skin colour rather than because of who she was. Outside college, however, it was a very different story.

*Third-year student, University of London*

It is important to remember that you shouldn't have to put up with being treated as different because of the colour of your skin or your background. You may think it will be difficult to prove you have been discriminated against. However, because of the work done in recent years in students' unions on promoting awareness, and the diversity of people who attend university, you will be able to find a sympathetic ear. Remember that a lot of racism stems from ignorance, so don't be afraid to tell someone their behaviour is offensive. If this doesn't stop them it is likely they are being intentionally racist and you should lodge a complaint with one of the organisations suggested above.

## Women at university

Women now represent 48 per cent of all students in the higher education system and many go through their entire university career without feeling as though they have been treated any differently from their male colleagues. However, sexism and sexual harassment, like all types of discrimination, come in many forms and are experienced in the higher education sector. If you are made to feel awkward by one of your lecturers, feel that your academic ability is being judged differently or that you are not being treated equally because you are a woman then you should definitely complain. You do not have to put up with sexual harassment or sexism and you have the right to be treated as seriously as any male student.

A friend of mine went to study engineering and ended up suffering from anorexia because she couldn't cope with the pressures of studying in such an overtly male environment. Her fellow students did little to welcome her and she felt totally isolated. Luckily she is a strong person and, last time I heard from her, she was recovering from anorexia and had stuck to her degree.

*First-year student, Brunel University*

If you feel you have experienced sexism or sexual harassment then you should go and talk to the women's officer in your students' union. She will be able to tell you how to pursue your complaint within the university. You should also talk to other women about what is happening to you; they might be having the same problems. It might also help to go to a women's group meeting to get the support of other women students. Women represent an extremely powerful force, especially when united against injustices suffered by fellow women.

We did a study here in Cardiff where we compared the degree results gained by women after anonymous marking had been introduced with those before it was implemented. The results were staggering. In 1985 when anonymous marking was introduced in the faculty of humanities, women started doing better: 47 per cent got firsts or upper seconds, which is roughly equal to their male counterparts. We are extremely happy with this system of marking by candidate numbers and would be horrified if we went back to the old system.

*Professor, Cardiff University*

# Being gay at university

Homophobia, like other forms of discrimination, stems from ignorance. You should not be put in a position where you are made to feel ashamed or are insulted because of your sexuality. Lesbianism, homosexuality and bisexuality are as valid forms of sexuality as heterosexuality and you should not have to tolerate other people's prejudices.

 I found that university really helped me to address my sexuality and come to terms with myself as a gay man. The lesbian, gay and bisexual support group was a really good place to meet like-minded people who helped me come out. But generally, I found that people who go through the higher education system tend to be more open-minded and more accepting of my sexual orientation.

*Welfare Officer, Lampeter University*

If you do become a victim of homophobia then you should go and talk to your students' union, either to the welfare officer or, if you feel happier talking to fellow homosexuals, the lesbian, gay and bisexual group or the lesbian and gay officer. Whatever you do, do not blame yourself. You do not have to put up with any form of homophobia and your union will be sympathetic to your experiences. Depending on the severity of your complaint, it will be able to speak to the harasser, ban them from the union or even implement a full disciplinary hearing involving the university. Unlike the outside world where the law is often vague or silent on the rights of gay men and lesbians, students' unions have set policies to protect their homosexual students so don't be afraid to speak out.

The National Union of Students runs a Gay and Lesbian Liberation Campaign which campaigns for equal rights for homosexual students. It hosts two conferences a year where gay and lesbian students from around the country meet to discuss issues and determine the direction the campaign should take. The NUS is bound by official policy to campaign for equal rights for homosexual students on the terms they suggest.

# Lifesavers⊗

## Organisations

Anti-Racist Alliance, PO Box 150, London WC1E 9AT, tel 071-278 6869.

Commission for Racial Equality (CRE), Eliot House, 10–12 Allington Street, London SW1E 5EH, tel 071-828 7022.

Equal Opportunities Commission, Overseas House, Quay Street, Manchester M3 3HN, tel 061-833 9244.

Gay and Lesbian Legal Advice (GLAD), tel 071-253 2043. Open Mon–Fri 7–9.30 pm. Provides a free telephone advice service for lesbians and gay men on legal matters and a referral service to local solicitors.

Lesbian and Gay Switchboard, tel 071-837 7324.

Lesbian Information Service, PO Box 8, Todmorden, Lancashire OL14 5TZ, tel 0706 817235. Provides an international information service.

Minority Rights Group Ltd, 379 Brixton Road, London SW9 7DE, tel 071-978 9498. Works to secure justice for minority or majority groups suffering discrimination.

Organisation for Lesbian and Gay Action, PO Box 147, London SE15 3SA. Campaigns for lesbian and gay rights and gives information to lesbian and gay groups and individuals.

Women Against Sexual Harassment (WASH), Suit 312, The Chandlery, 50 Westminster Bridge Road, London SE1 7QY, tel 071-721 7592. Gives advice, including free legal advice, over the phone and face to face.

# Glossary

**Access funds** Sums of money which universities give to their students who are facing particular hardship, providing they meet certain individual university-set criteria.

**Campus** The area where the university buildings are. Some campuses also have accommodation buildings on site and are completely self-contained centres of student life.

**Chancellor** Usually a nominal 'head' of the university, brought out on ceremonial occasions to shake hands and pass on congratulations. To make things more confusing, this person is sometimes also known as a Visitor.

**Dean of Students** The person, if one exists in your university, responsible for your welfare – both academic and personal.

**Department** The part of the university responsible for teaching your course. You can be a member of more than one department if you are on a joint course.

**Director of Studies** Also known as the Head of Department, which is much more self-explanatory. Basically the person responsible for carrying out the administration of a department. He or she will probably do some teaching as well.

**Discretionary grant** The additional sum of money some students with special needs or who don't qualify for a mandatory grant may receive. It depends entirely on how generous the LEA is feeling and how persuasive you are.

**Executive Officers** Elected students there to help the sabbaticals with anything from making posters to representing student views to the university.

**Faculty** The umbrella organisation for related departments. The Arts faculty carries out the administration for the humanities subjects and the Science faculty, the science subjects.

**Freshers** The term used to describe all first-year students. You will definitely get cheesed off with being called a fresher two terms into your first year by 'mature' second-year students. Ignore them: 12 months from now you'll be doing the same to next year's intake.

**Freshers' fairs** Events where the local banks, businesses and students' union clubs and societies all try to persuade you that they are the best thing since sliced bread.

**General Union Meetings** These come under a variety of titles but are basically where students of the university decide what policy the students' union should adopt. Where politically motivated students get the chance to practise the oratory techniques they one day hope to employ in the House of Commons, while their fellow students shout them down.

**Halls** Halls of residence are buildings where students (usually first years) live.

**Lecturer** A member of a department who gives lectures. He or she probably has a specialist field and researches it when not teaching.

**Mandatory grant** The pitiful amount of money students are given through their LEAs. All full-time students studying for a first degree or equivalent qualify, but the amount you get will be judged on your parents' income.

**The National Union of Students (NUS)** The national representative student body. Currently, you are automatically a member of NUS if your university is affiliated (and most are).

**Overdrafts** Money you arrange to borrow from the bank to keep you off the breadline. You have to pay them back when you graduate, with interest added.

**Parental contribution** The amount your parents are asked to fork out so you can live, if their salaries mean you don't get a full mandatory grant.

**Personal tutor** The tutor in your department who has been assigned to look after your welfare. He or she may or may not be the tutor who teaches you.

**Rag** Where students do silly things and have a lot of fun all in the name of raising money for charity. Also can be a derogatory, or perhaps affectionate, term for the student newspaper.

**The registry** Unusually for universities, this is actually the place where you go to register as a student. It is also the place you go to pick up your grant and fill out your student loan application forms.

**Sabbatical officers** Elected from, and by, the students at the university and paid a salary to take responsibility for running aspects of the students' union. They are very well versed on student issues as they have recent experience of being a student in your university.

**Seminars** Group discussions with a lecturer where you will probably have to take your courage in both hands and present a paper in front of the class.

**Student loans** The money you can borrow from the Student Loans Company during your time at university to supplement your grant or parental contribution. You have to pay it back when you graduate, with interest added.

**Students' unions** Also known as guilds of students, student associations and junior common rooms. The places that provide cheap beer, entertainments, clubs, societies, stationery, food and can help you with any problem you might possibly encounter in complete confidence. Centres of information, advice and support.

**Tutor** The person who teaches you individually or with a small group of other people in a tutorial or a seminar.

**Vice-Chancellor** If you have a VC, then he or she will be the big boss who does all the hard work and is responsible for running the university. It gets confusing because these people also go under the titles of Principal, Director or Dean. It depends on what basis your university was set up.

**Vice-Principal** The deputy to the VC.

**Welfare Officer** The sabbatical officer and/or member of staff who is responsible for the welfare of all the students at the university. Very helpful, totally unshockable people who have seen it all before. They are the first point of contact for any difficulties you have while you are at university.

# General Directory

Your primary source of information and advice will be your students' union and/or your university. There will also be local specialist organisations listed in the phone book who will be able to give you specific advice or refer you to groups in your area.

The following organisations are listed because they are the headquarters of groups you might encounter, or need help from, during your time at university.

Department for Education, Sanctuary Buildings, Great Smith Street, London SW1P 3BT, tel 071-925 5000.

National Association of Citizens' Advice Bureaux (NACAB), 115–123 Pentonville Road, London N1 9LZ, tel 071-833 4731.

National Union of Students, Mandela House, 461 Holloway Road, London N7 6LJ, tel 071-272 8900.

Samaritans Local numbers are given in the front of phone books.

The Universities and Colleges Admissions Service (UCAS), PO Box 28, Cheltenham, Gloucestershire GL50 3SA, tel 0242 222444.

United Kingdom Council for Overseas Student Affairs (UKCOSA), 9–17 St Alban's Place, London NI 0NX, tel 071-226 3762.